**American Forum for Global Education**
**World Studies Series**
Edited by Ria Boemi

1. Joseph D. Wilcox, *A Middle East Primer for Students*. 2004.

# A Middle East Primer
# for Students

*American Forum for Global Education*
*World Studies Series, No. 1*

Joseph D. Wilcox

Published in partnership with the
American Forum for Global Education

ScarecrowEducation
Lanham, Maryland • Toronto • Oxford
2004

Published in partnership with the
American Forum for Global Education

Published in the United States of America
by ScarecrowEducation
An imprint of The Rowman & Littlefield Publishing Group, Inc.
4501 Forbes Boulevard, Suite 200, Lanham, Maryland 20706
www.scarecroweducation.com

PO Box 317
Oxford
OX2 9RU, UK

British Library Cataloguing in Publication Information Available

**Library of Congress Cataloging-in-Publication Data**
Wilcox, Joseph D., 1965–
    A Middle East primer for students / Joseph D. Wilcox.
        p. cm. — (American Forum for Global Education. World studies series ;
no. 1)
    Includes bibliographical references.
    ISBN 1-57886-163-2 (pbk. : alk. paper)
    1. Middle East. I. Title. II. Series.
DS44.W635 2004
956—dc22
                                                    2004008161

♾ ™ The paper used in this publication meets the minimum requirements of
American National Standard for Information Sciences—Permanence of
Paper for Printed Library Materials, ANSI/NISO Z39.48–1992.
Manufactured in the United States of America.

# Contents

Acknowledgments                vii
Map of the Middle East       viii

**1** The Middle East Today       1
   Cradle of Civilization     2
   Major Challenges for the Region   3
   Young People of the Middle East   5

**2** Geography of the Middle East   7
   Regions of the Middle East   7
   Quest for Water   9
   Facts and Figures: Geography   11
   Study Questions   18

**3** History of the Middle East   19
   Prehistory: 8500 to 300 B.C.   19
   Era of Empire: 550 B.C. to 1920 A.D.   22
   Conflict and Strife: 1920 to 2004   27
   The Arab–Israeli Conflict   28
   The Gulf Wars   31
   Islamic Fundamentalism   33
   Study Questions   35

**4** Economics   37
   The Cost of Unrest   37
   The "Freedom Deficit"   38
   The Cost of Poor Education   39

The Middle East's Burgeoning Youth                    39
Big Oil                                               40
Signs of Improvement                                 40
Facts and Figures: People                            41
Study Questions                                      48

5  Issues of Identity                                49
Arab Nationalism                                     49
Religion                                             51
Spotlight on Saudi Arabia                            58
Conclusion                                           60
Study Questions                                      61

Appendix A: Middle East Time Line                    63

Appendix B: Internet Resources                       67

Glossary                                             69

Bibliography                                         71

About the Author                                     73

# Acknowledgments

While writing this text I consulted many sources, but I would like to offer a special thanks to *National Geographic* magazine and the National Geographic book *Cradle & Crucible: History and Faith in the Middle East* by David Fromkin et al. *National Geographic* and its writers provided me with many insights and learning opportunities.

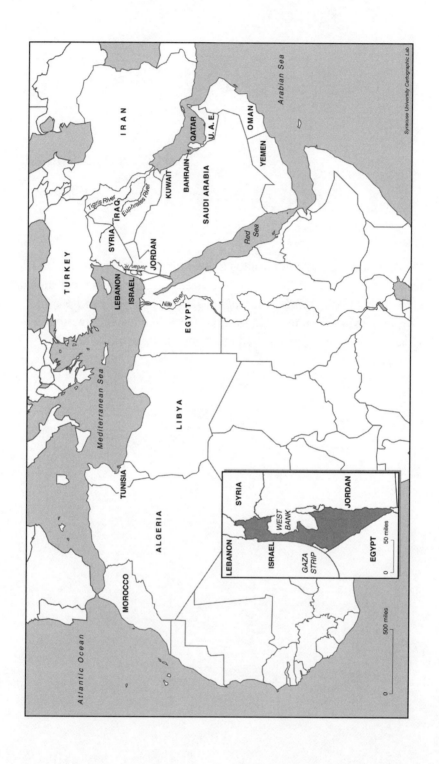

# CHAPTER 1

# The Middle East Today

One look at Saudi Arabia during the month of Ramadan and it's easy to see that the Middle East has an identity complex. At 3:30 in the morning, young men in jeans and baseball caps cruise in American cars alongside chauffeured young girls in veils and traditional black gowns known as *abayas*. At stoplights, girls shower the boys' cars with wadded up paper balls, each containing a cell-phone number. The practice of "numbering" and cell-phone dating is just one example of how Arabs negotiate the modern world in a society bound by age-old traditions (Viviano, 2003).

Although traditions rooted in Islam influence much of the Middle East, a closer look reveals that a rich dichotomy colors the region. For example, in Israel, Judaism is predominant and in Turkey, which is Islamic, a secular form of rule provides its citizens with more religious freedom than in some other Middle Eastern countries where women have been sentenced to death by stoning for violating Islamic law. The Middle East is a region in search of itself and the outcome of this struggle will profoundly impact the United States and the world.

But what are Middle Easterners searching for and why has that search been seemingly mired in conflict and strife in recent times? Most Americans know the Middle East only as a crucible, where images of war flash across televisions and cover the front pages of newspapers. Lying squarely between Europe, Africa, and Asia, the Middle East—a fitting name for a region washed by the waves of the Mediterranean Sea (from the Latin *medius* for "middle" and *terra* for "land")—has also been at the center of a long-running struggle between the East and West that is once again at the forefront of world politics. What happens in this region is central not only to U.S. prosperity and security but also to the prosperity and security of much of the world.

In January 2004, Al Jazeera, the Arab version of CNN in the United States, broadcast a video statement allegedly made by Osama bin Laden. In the tape, bin Laden calls the coalition troops in Baghdad "crusaders," harking back to the East–West clash that stems from the eleventh century when the Catholic pope called on Westerners to embark on a crusade to liberate Jerusalem from the grip of Islam. Of course, Osama bin Laden is an extremist and does not represent popular opinion in the Middle East. If we got all of our information about the Middle East from television and newspapers, we might think everyone in the Middle East is a terrorist but that is absolutely false.

Our aim with this book is to root students in a basic understanding of the Middle East, its history and its peoples; to show how that history continues to resonate; and to investigate why the United States would want to fight two wars in the region, in 1991 and again in 2003. In addition, we aim to show where the Middle East fits into the modern world and how important the region is to world stability and prosperity.

## CRADLE OF CIVILIZATION

Although some think of this land as the region that nurtured Osama bin Laden and Saddam Hussein, the Middle East is the cradle of civilization, a place where people first promoted the notion of monotheism, the belief in a single, almighty God. The three great monotheistic religions are Judaism, Christianity, and Islam, with the latter two faiths claiming more followers than any other faith in the world. Religion is just one of many contributions the Middle East has presented to humanity, and one of the strongest forces shaping the world is the relationship between these three great faiths.

In addition, the people of the Middle East created agriculture and developed the world's first writing systems, were the first to use the wheel, and gave us our system of measuring time by 60-second intervals. And while Europe lumbered slowly forward from about 476 to 1000 A.D., the Middle East had already accomplished spectacular feats of art, engineering, and science.

Although this region has a long, rich history, historians have not always been fair to the region. Often historians have emphasized Europe and Asia while the story of the Arabs often seems to get lost in the dust left behind by the armies and empires that have invaded and conquered these lands from antiquity to the present. At the end of World War I, European powers dismantled the Ottoman Empire, which ruled over the region for some 500 years, and remapped the region, calling it the Middle East. Until then, many preferred to use the terms the Near East or Western Asia and some still use these terms.

For our purposes, the Middle East can be defined as a region stretching east from the Mediterranean Sea to Iran and encompassing all of the Arabian Peninsula and parts of North Africa. It is roughly the size of the United States with 230 million people, which is about 60 million fewer than the population of America. However, some define the region much more broadly, stretching as far east as India and covering some African countries like Somalia and Mauritania. No matter what definition one uses, there's no denying several major challenges that are part of the Middle Eastern fabric.

## MAJOR CHALLENGES FOR THE REGION

### War and Strife

In 1991 and again in 2003, the United States fought two major wars in the Middle East against Iraq. The 2003 war, meant to topple Saddam Hussein and rid him of his weapons of mass destruction, had a major impact on the U.S. presidential and other national elections in 2004. The choice made by Prime Minister Tony Blair of Great Britain to ally with the United States also challenged his leadership. And historians will likely debate the legacy of this war for years to come.

The Arab–Israeli conflict is also a major challenge. The roots of this ongoing battle stretch back thousands of years, to be woven into the fabric of the region. This conflict has the capacity, as one famous journalist observed, to influence not only the destiny of the region but perhaps the destiny of the world. Since the creation of the state of Israel in 1948, Israel and her neighbors have battled several times over the Jews' historical and religious right to live in the Holy Land abutting the Mediterranean Sea.

**Oil and Terrorism**

Oil poses another major challenge. Although discovery of this black gold has been a major boon for the Middle East, it has caused some major headaches. Oil has enriched some countries in this region but it has also led to vast gaps between rich and poor countries in the region as well as ever-widening gaps between the rich and poor within oil-producing states.

Many say oil is one of the major reasons why the United States invests so much time and energy in the Middle East, and since September 11, 2001, that investment has become more important than ever. The Middle East has become the central battleground in worldwide efforts by the United States' and other countries to root out terrorism. Four of the seven countries the U.S. Department of State lists as sponsors and exporters of terrorism are in the Middle East: Libya, Syria, Iran, and Iraq (the others are Sudan, Cuba, and North Korea). Fifteen of the nineteen al-Qaida terrorists who hijacked four American planes and crashed them in New York, Washington, D.C., and Pennsylvania were Saudi Arabian. Other terrorists attacks against the United States include:

- 1998 and 2001—Al-Qaida bombed two U.S. embassies and a U.S. warship in Africa.
- 1996—Islamic fundamentalists backed by Iran bombed a U.S. military residence in Saudi Arabia.
- 1993—An extremist Islamic group bombed the World Trade Center.
- 1988—An American airliner was bombed as it flew over Lockerbie, Scotland, killing 270 people. In 2002, a Libyan intelligence officer was convicted of carrying out the bombing and Libya agreed to pay survivors' families millions of dollars in damages.
- 1983—An Iranian-backed group killed 241 U.S. Marines, sailors, and soldiers after driving a truck bomb into a U.S. military compound in Lebanon.

Since the 1980s, tens of thousands of people have been killed or wounded in terrorist attacks against U.S. targets. Terrorists target the United States as well as the governments of several Middle East countries for many reasons.

In some specific circumstances, terrorists have targeted the United States over its involvement in the Arab–Israeli conflict. On a more general level, many fundamentalist Islamic extremists resent any U.S. presence in the Middle East because they believe Western influence interferes with their way of life and their desire to create strict Islamic regimes, where everything from social customs to criminal law is based on the teachings of the Koran.

The thread of this conflict between Western powers and Islamic faithful in the Middle East can be traced back to the Crusades in the eleventh century, when Pope Urban II urged Christians to rescue Jerusalem from the Muslim presence. It's important for us to understand that for thousands of years the East and West have clashed and coexisted in this region and often the differences have been based on religion. Whenever Osama bin Laden urges his followers to fight, he laces his oratory with Islamic symbols and rhetoric of Islamic glory over Western "infidels" who have sullied Middle Eastern soil.

It must be noted that Osama bin Laden preaches a virulent brand of Islamic fundamentalism based on his reading of history. Most Muslims do not support the way in which bin Laden interprets the Koran. In addition, as we shall see, Islamic fundamentalism poses grave internal problems for many Middle Eastern countries. Islamic extremists have assassinated Middle Eastern leaders and many internal problems faced by governments in the region are intertwined with the recent rise of Islamic fundamentalism.

## YOUNG PEOPLE OF THE MIDDLE EAST

Education is another major dilemma for the Middle East, especially when looked at in light of how quickly the under-20 population in the region has grown in recent years. Many Middle Eastern countries lack the resources to educate their young people; some countries have offered little training that would prepare a modern workforce to compete in the global marketplace. Literacy rates range from about 40 percent in Yemen to 95 percent in Israel. More than half the illiterate in the Middle East are women.

A deep sense of frustration among some people in the Middle East, especially the young, poses a major problem, a problem that is due in large part to the region's lagging economy, delayed efforts to democratize, and the large numbers of displaced people throughout the region. The wave of democracy in the 1980s and 1990s that swept through Latin America, East Asia, Central Asia, and Eastern Europe barely reached these Arab countries. This "freedom deficit," as the United Nations and some Arab scholars refer to it, undermines human development as well as economic and political progress for much of the region. The lack of economic growth in most of the region also hobbled the Middle East.

The Middle East receives a lot of attention from the media and politicians for the strife that has roiled the region and the virulent brand of terrorism it has exported. But to truly understand this part of the world is to understand that its peoples have contributed greatly to civilization. Middle East and Arab contributions impact nearly all aspects of our daily lives. From our homes, offices, and schools to religion, philosophy, arts, and science, we are indebted to the ingenuity and creativity of Middle Eastern peoples. The Middle East has always been a great cauldron of societies and cultures where rapid expansion by empires and traders helped weld together many peoples, including Arabians, Africans, Berbers, Egyptians, Phoenicians, and Europeans. This dynamic mixing of peoples helped create a vibrant region.

# CHAPTER 2

# Geography of the Middle East

Popular film and media might lead one to think that the Middle East is Lawrence of Arabia charging across Saudi Arabian deserts, where nomads wander endless, parched landscapes ringed by shimmering mirages. In reality, natural forces carved quite a varied landscape in the Middle East, ranging from bountiful rivers to lifeless salt-crusted flats, to high, jagged mountains and flat plateaus to deserts, where temperatures soar to over 130 degrees Fahrenheit, to mountains capped by permanent snowfields and glaciers.

## REGIONS OF THE MIDDLE EAST

### The Northern Region

Huge mountains running through Turkey and Iran form the northern region. Here, the Bosporus and Dardanelles on the western edge of the Anatolian Peninsula in Turkey separate the Middle East from Europe. These straits also lead from the Black Sea in the north of this region to the Mediterranean Sea in the south. Permanent snowfields and glaciers cover the slopes of Mount Ararat in eastern Turkey and Mount Damavand in Iran.

The Kurds, an ethnic minority, live in the mountainous northern region in Turkey, Iraq, and Iran. Although there are no official boundaries, the Kurds have long maintained that they should have their own homeland in this region.

## The Fertile Crescent

Another region is the Fertile Crescent, perhaps the most well-known and most studied region of the Middle East. It loops from the Mediterranean coastal areas of southern Israel northward through Lebanon, then east through Syria and Iraq, and southward to the Persian Gulf. Its name derived from its shape and from the Tigris and Euphrates rivers, rivers that sustained the world's first agricultural systems and the first known civilizations and cosmopolitan centers.

## The Arabian Peninsula

The Arabian Peninsula is home to Saudi Arabia and several smaller states. The region is primarily desert and it houses the world's richest oil and natural gas deposits. Recent estimates by the U.S. Geological Survey (USGS) and by the Middle East journal *World Oil* show that the Middle East contains anywhere from 40 to 66 percent of the world's oil reserves. (The USGS says reserves are about 40 percent while Middle East oil producers claim the total is about 66 percent.) This concentration of natural resources enriched some countries and their citizens; countries that don't produce oil have a smaller share of Middle East wealth. The one exception in the region might be Israel, which maintains a higher standard of living yet has no oil reserves. But like all resources, oil wells in the Middle East will eventually run dry, faster in some countries than in others, and most leaders in this region have struggled to find other sources of income and to expand their economies and industries in order to decrease dependence on oil.

Going counterclockwise from the northwest, the Arabian Peninsula is ringed by the Red Sea, the Gulf of Aden, the Arabian Sea, the Indian Ocean, and the Persian Gulf. In addition to parched deserts, mountains also dot Yemen and other coastal areas in the eastern and southwestern corners. Bahrain, an island in the Red Sea, is also part of this region.

## North Africa

North Africa comprises the fourth major region of the Middle East; like the Arabian Peninsula, it is mostly an arid, sandy environment covered primarily by the Sahara Desert. However, parts of the Mediterranean coastlines are quite lush and support the production of date palms, wheat, and other agriculture. Also, the occasional oasis and the Nile River, with its fertile delta emptying into the Mediterranean Sea, break up the Sahara's parched sands.

## QUEST FOR WATER

The Middle East covers an area nearly equal to the size of the United States and its population is on par with America's 290 million people. Yet only about 3 percent of the Middle East receives enough rain to sustain agriculture and some deserts in Saudi Arabia and Egypt can go years without rainfall (Kort, 2002). That translates to about half an acre of arable land per person in the Middle East, compared to 1.5 acres per person in the United States (Kort, 2002). Although some Middle Eastern countries grow surplus food supplies and can export some crops—for example, Turkey with its wheat production—others rely heavily on food imports. Kuwait, for example, must import all of its food and a great deal of its water.

For many, life in the Middle East is a constant quest for water. Parts of Iraq, Iran, Turkey, the Mediterranean coastal areas of Syria, Israel, and Lebanon, and the mountains of Yemen receive regular rainfall, but even in these areas water is often scarce. Such scarcities often lead to bitter disputes—for example, in the Arab–Israeli conflict, where water rights have been a major issue in the search for peace.

### Major Rivers

Some rivers in the Middle East flow only during certain times of the year and are dry the rest of the time, while others are plentiful. The Tigris and Euphrates rivers supply an adequate amount of water for those living in the Fertile Crescent, and the Nile brings enough water for those living near its banks. The lands between the Tigris and Euphrates supported a series of great civilizations, beginning with Sumeria. This area is known as Mesopotamia, which in Greek means "between the rivers."

However, few other areas of the Middle East—besides parts of Israel, which receives water from the Jordan River, and parts of Iran, Yemen, Turkey, Syria, and Lebanon—receive adequate rainfall. Compared to the Nile or the waters of the Tigris-Euphrates, the Jordan is a mere trickle. In some parts of the Middle East, including Iran, Turkey, and Yemen, rain falls primarily in winter. In the southern regions of the Middle East, including the Arabian Peninsula and North Africa, typical annual rainfall amounts are about 4 inches (Kort, 2002).

## Oases

Another important source of water in the Middle East is groundwater. These aquifers have supplied oases for centuries. In recent years, Saudi Arabia and Libya have also found "new" pools of groundwater beneath desert sands. Some of these underground pools are left over from the last ice age, where water seeped through the soil and settled between rock formations. Once these water sources are depleted, they cannot be renewed and must be managed carefully (McCoy, 2003).

## Dams

Damming rivers in some Middle Eastern countries, most notably in Egypt and Turkey, helped increase the amount of arable land, but the dams have also led to other environmental problems and disputes. Turkey's Southeastern Anatolia Project (GAP Project, as it's known in Turkey) envisions the building of 22 dams and 19 power plants along the Tigris and Euphrates rivers. However, Syria and Iraq, downstream from the dams, claim the dams block their water rights. The ambitious GAP Project, due to be completed in 2005, will expand Turkey's irrigated land by 40 percent. Since much of the Tigris and Euphrates rivers run through lightly populated regions, proponents of the project say it will help distribute much needed water to people in more heavily populated areas.

The Middle East offers a truly diverse landscape, from snowcapped mountains to vast dry deserts that can reach 130 degrees Fahrenheit. As we shall see, this varied landscape has also played a major role in shaping Middle East history and its place in the world.

## FACTS AND FIGURES: GEOGRAPHY

### Northern Tier Countries

*Iran*

**Location:** borders the Gulf of Oman, the Persian Gulf, and the Caspian Sea; between Iraq and Pakistan

**Total area:** 636,293 square miles; 1.6 million square km; slightly larger than Alaska

**Climate:** mostly arid or semiarid, subtropical along Caspian coast

**Terrain:** rugged, mountainous rim; high, central basin with deserts, mountains; small, discontinuous plains along both coasts

**Arable land:** 10.17%

*Turkey*

**Location:** southeastern Europe and southwestern Asia (that portion of Turkey west of the Bosporus is geographically part of Europe); borders the Black Sea, between Bulgaria and Georgia, and bordering the Aegean Sea and the Mediterranean Sea, between Greece and Syria

**Total area:** 301,382 square miles; 780,580 square km; slightly larger than Texas

**Climate:** temperate; hot, dry summers with mild, wet winters; harsher in interior

**Terrain:** mostly mountains; narrow coastal plain; high central plateau (Anatolia)

**Arable land:** 34.53%

### Fertile Crescent Countries

*Iraq*

**Location:** borders the Persian Gulf, between Iran and Kuwait

**Total area:** 168,754 square miles; 437,072 square km; about twice the size of Idaho

**Climate:** mostly desert; mild to cool winters with dry, hot, cloudless summers; northern mountainous regions along Iranian and Turkish borders experience cold winters with occasionally heavy snows that melt in early spring, sometimes causing extensive flooding in central and Southern Iraq

**Terrain:** mostly broad plains; reedy marshes along Iranian border in south with large flooded areas; mountains along borders with Iran and Turkey

**Arable land:** 11.9%

## *Israel*

**Location:** borders the Mediterranean Sea, between Egypt and Lebanon

**Total area:** 8,019 square miles; 20,770 square km; slightly smaller than New Jersey

**Climate:** temperate; hot and dry in southern and eastern desert areas

**Terrain:** Negev Desert in the south; low coastal plain; central mountains; Jordan Rift Valley

**Arable land:** 17%

## *Lebanon*

**Location:** borders the Mediterranean Sea, between Israel and Syria

**Total area:** 4,016 square miles; 10,400 square km; 0.7 times the size of Connecticut

**Climate:** Mediterranean; mild to cool, wet winters with hot, dry summers; Lebanon Mountains experience heavy winter snows

**Terrain:** narrow coastal plain; El Beqaa (Bekaa Valley) separates Lebanon and Anti-Lebanon Mountains

**Arable land:** 17.6%

## *Syria*

**Location:** borders the Mediterranean Sea, between Lebanon and Turkey

**Total area:** 71,498 square miles; 185,180 square km; slightly larger than North Dakota

**Climate:** mostly desert; hot, dry, sunny summers (June to August) and mild, rainy winters (December to February) along coast; cold weather with snow or sleet periodically in Damascus

**Terrain:** primarily semiarid and desert plateau; narrow coastal plain; mountains in west
**Arable land:** 26%

### Arabian Peninsula

#### *Bahrain*

**Location:** archipelago in the Persian Gulf, east of Saudi Arabia
**Total area:** 257 square miles; 665 square km; 3.5 times the size of Washington, D.C.
**Climate:** arid; mild, pleasant winters; very hot, humid summers
**Terrain:** mostly low desert plain rising gently to low central escarpment
**Arable land:** 4.35%

#### *Jordan*

**Location:** northwest of Saudi Arabia
**Total area:** 35,637 square miles; 92,300 square km; slightly smaller than Indiana
**Climate:** mostly arid desert; rainy season in west (November to April)
**Terrain:** mostly desert plateau in east, highland area in west; Great Rift Valley separates East and West Banks of the Jordan River
**Arable land:** 2.9%

#### *Kuwait*

**Location:** borders the Persian Gulf, between Iraq and Saudi Arabia
**Total area:** 6,880 square miles; 17,820 square km; slightly smaller than New Jersey
**Climate:** dry desert; intensely hot summers; short, cool winters
**Terrain:** flat to slightly undulating desert plain
**Arable land:** 0.34%

#### *Oman*

**Location:** borders the Arabian Sea, Gulf of Oman, and Persian Gulf; between Yemen and United Arab Emirates

**Total area:** 82,031 square miles; 212,460 square km; slightly smaller than Kansas

**Climate:** dry desert; hot, humid along coast; hot, dry interior; strong southwest summer monsoon (May to September) in far south

**Terrain:** central desert plain, rugged mountains in north and south

**Arable land:** 0.08%

## *Qatar*

**Location:** borders the Persian Gulf and Saudi Arabia

**Total area:** 4,416 square miles; 11,437 square km; slightly smaller than Connecticut

**Climate:** arid; mild, pleasant winters; very hot, humid summers

**Terrain:** mostly flat and barren desert covered with loose sand and gravel

**Arable land:** 1.3%

## *Saudi Arabia*

**Location:** borders the Persian Gulf and the Red Sea, north of Yemen

**Total area:** 756,981 square miles; 1.96 million square km; about one-fifth the size of the United States.

**Climate:** harsh, dry desert with great temperature extremes

**Terrain:** mostly uninhabited, sandy desert

**Arable land:** 1.7%

## *United Arab Emirates*

**Location:** borders the Gulf of Oman and the Persian Gulf, between Oman and Saudi Arabia

**Total area:** 32,000 square miles; 82,880 square km; smaller than Maine

**Climate:** desert; cooler in eastern mountains

**Terrain:** flat, barren coastal plain merging into rolling sand dunes of vast desert wasteland; mountains in east

**Arable land:** 0.5%

## *Yemen*

**Location:** borders the Arabian Sea, Gulf of Aden, and Red Sea; between Oman and Saudi Arabia

**Total area:** 203,846 square miles; 527,970 square km; slightly larger than twice the size of Wyoming

**Climate:** mostly desert; hot and humid along west coast; temperate in western mountains affected by seasonal monsoon; extraordinarily hot, dry, harsh desert in east

**Terrain:** narrow coastal plain backed by flat-topped hills and rugged mountains; dissected upland desert plains in center slope into the desert interior of the Arabian Peninsula

**Arable land:** 2.8%

## North Africa

### *Algeria*

**Location:** borders the Mediterranean Sea, between Morocco and Tunisia

**Total area:** 919,590 square miles; 2.4 million square km; about 3.5 times larger than Texas

**Climate:** arid to semiarid; mild, wet winters with hot, dry summers along coast; drier with cold winters and hot summers on high plateau; sirocco is a hot, dust/sand-laden wind especially common in summer

**Terrain:** mostly high plateau and desert; some mountains; narrow, discontinuous coastal plain

**Arable land:** 3.2%

### *Egypt*

**Location:** borders the Mediterranean Sea; between Libya and the Gaza Strip, and the Red Sea north of Sudan; includes the Asian Sinai Peninsula

**Total area:** 386,660 square miles; 1 million square km; slightly three times the size of New Mexico

**Climate:** desert; hot, dry summers with moderate winters

**Terrain:** vast desert plateau interrupted by Nile valley and delta
**Arable land:** 2.9%

## Libya

**Location:** borders the Mediterranean Sea, between Egypt and Tunisia
**Total area:** 679,358 square miles; 1.8 million square km; slightly
  larger than Alaska
**Climate:** Mediterranean along coast; dry, extreme desert interior
**Terrain:** mostly barren, flat to undulating plains, plateaus, depressions
**Arable land:** 1%

## Morocco

**Location:** borders the North Atlantic Ocean and the Mediterranean
  Sea, between Algeria and Western Sahara
**Total area:** 172,413 square miles; 446,550 square km; slightly larger
  than California
**Climate:** Mediterranean, becoming more extreme in the interior
**Terrain:** northern coast and interior are mountainous with large areas
  of bordering plateaus, valleys, and rich coastal plains
**Arable land:** 20%

## Palestine (Gaza Strip)

**Location:** borders the Mediterranean Sea, between Egypt and Israel
**Total area:** 223 square miles; 360 square km; more than twice the size
  of Washington, D.C.
**Climate:** temperate, mild winters, dry and warm to hot summers
**Terrain:** flat to rolling, sand- and dune-covered coastal plain
**Arable land:** 26%

## Palestine (West Bank)

**Location:** west of Jordan
**Total area:** 3,633 square miles; 5,860 square km; slightly smaller than
  Delaware

**Climate:** temperate; temperature and precipitation vary with altitude, warm to hot summers, cool to mild winters

**Terrain:** mostly rugged dissected upland, some vegetation in west, but barren in east

**Arable land:** negligible

## *Tunisia*

**Location:** borders the Mediterranean Sea, between Algeria and Libya

**Total area:** 63,170 square miles; 163,610 square km; slightly larger than the state of Georgia

**Climate:** temperate in north with mild, rainy winters and hot, dry summers; desert in south

**Terrain:** mountains in north; hot, dry central plain; semiarid south merges into the Sahara

**Arable land:** 18.7%

## *United States*

**Location:** North America, bordering both the North Atlantic Ocean and the North Pacific Ocean, between Canada and Mexico

**Total area:** 5,970,036 square miles; 9,629,091 square km; about half the size of Russia; about three-tenths the size of Africa; about half the size of South America (or slightly larger than Brazil); slightly larger than China; about two and a half times the size of Western Europe

**Climate:** mostly temperate, but tropical in Hawaii and Florida, arctic in Alaska, semiarid in the great plains west of the Mississippi River, and arid in the Great Basin of the southwest; low winter temperatures in the northwest are ameliorated occasionally in January and February by warm Chinook winds from the eastern slopes of the Rocky Mountains

**Terrain:** vast central plain, mountains in west, hills and low mountains in east; rugged mountains and broad river valleys in Alaska; rugged, volcanic topography in Hawaii

**Arable land:** 19.3%

Source: *CIA World Factbook,* 2003

## STUDY QUESTIONS

1. How has this chapter on geography changed your impression of the Middle East's landscape?
2. How large is the Middle East in relation to the United States? Approximately how many people live in the Middle East?
3. What are the Middle East's major geographic regions? Compare and contrast the regions. What desert covers a large portion of North Africa?
4. What are some of the major rivers in the Middle East? How have these rivers influenced Middle East history and the history of civilization? In what ways do these rivers continue to shape the Middle East? What is another important source of water in the Middle East?
5. What is arable land? If you were the leader of a country that had no arable land or freshwater sources, how would you provide food and water for your people?

# CHAPTER 3

# History of the Middle East

## PREHISTORY: 8500 TO 300 B.C.

The Middle East is the cradle of civilization, which started in the Fertile Crescent, an area sweeping up from southern Israel, eastward through Syria and Iraq, and curving back down to the Persian Gulf. The region contains life-giving sources of water—the Nile, Jordan, Tigris, and Euphrates rivers—as well as a hospitable climate and rich soils. Here, about 12,000 years ago in Canaan (modern Israel), the first permanent settlements appeared. These early settlers primarily foraged and hunted but over thousands of years they learned to domesticate plants and animals. The processes of domesticating plants and animals may seem simple in our modern times but they were the keys that freed people from antiquity and launched them into the realm of civilization.

With these innovations, over thousands of years, small villages would grow into city-states then expand into nations. As we shall see, this growth was not organic. It was a reaction to many outside forces such as the need for resources and the nations' desires to defend themselves against invaders. By 1000 B.C., powerful leaders began vying for control over the Middle East and North Africa, and what was once a loose network of small villages grew into a world interconnected by trade and the desire for empire.

Some believe hunter-gatherers began to domesticate plants and animals because the communities that foraged off the land grew quite large, perhaps with populations in the thousands, and they needed a more dependable and plentiful food supply (Fromkin et al., 2003). Two to three thousand years after settlers appeared at Canaan, large communities in

Syria, Anatolia (modern Turkey), Iraq, and Iran, usually living near lakeshores and rivers, herded sheep and goats, and cultivated grains and nuts. By the sixth millennium B.C., farming had also spread to the Nile Valley (Fromkin et al., 2003).

## Roots of Urbanism

Nevertheless, farming communities dotted the Middle East, with some populations numbering into the thousands. Women primarily managed agricultural and household chores, while men most likely hunted wild game and herded flocks of domesticated animals. As these centers grew more wealthy and complex, a class of artisans emerged and began to develop stone tools from flint and pottery from clay, which people used to store food and water. Some of the earliest societies began developing artwork as well, often clay figures depicting humans and animals. The figures formed the basis of religion and people ascribed great powers to the figures, the power to ensure fertility and to guarantee bountiful harvests (Fromkin et al., 2003).

By the sixth millennium B.C., many farming communities had also developed weaving and irrigation and maintained surplus supplies of food and other goods. The surpluses were important because they freed some people from the daily routine of farming, and eventually, traders, craftsmen, nomadic herders, and elites began to emerge. Vast trade networks also began to connect cultures throughout the Fertile Crescent.

By the fourth millennium B.C., a new urban lifestyle developed in societies like Mesopotamia and Egypt and marked the beginning of civilization. One of these groups was known as the Sumerians. By 3100 B.C., they established a capital at Ur on the Euphrates River in southern Iraq and ruled over much of Mesopotamia. About 24,000 people lived inside the walled city of Ur, which covered about 240 acres, an impressive urban center. At the same time, others built urban centers along the Mediterranean shores, in Syria, Anatolia, and Iran.

By 3000 B.C., Egypt established a vast kingdom stretching along the Nile River from the Mediterranean to deep inside the interior near Aswan in the south. Around 2500 B.C., the kingdom of Elam emerged in western Iran. Bloody battles and skirmishes defined the relationship among the urban centers springing up throughout the Fertile Crescent. At the same time, powerful leaders and ruling classes emerged, wielding enormous power over their respective peoples. Societies grew increasingly stratified, with the concentration of wealth belonging to elites and kings and military leaders, who ruled by coercion and by divine authority. Sumerian kings claimed to have been appointed by gods, and in Egypt, followers considered their rulers to be gods and goddesses (Fromkin et al, 2003).

One consequence of the relationship between the ruler and the ruled was the large number of people forced to join armies and build temples, monuments, and pyramids. In Ur and in Egypt, archeological evidence suggests some slaves were even sacrificed and buried with their leaders to serve them in the afterlife.

### Writing Systems, Technology, and Empire

Eventually, around 3100 B.C., the Sumerians developed cuneiform writing to help them maintain administrative control over increasingly complex economic and political systems. Egyptians also invented hieroglyphs to record accounts of land ownership, surpluses and trade, and to maintain calendars. Although the first cuneiform writing systems were used solely for administrative purposes (i.e., recording debts and business transactions), a few centuries later the Sumerians and other societies used writing to record history and to develop legal codes and scientific endeavors such as mathematics and astronomy. The first forms of literature emerged as well.

During the fourth and third millennia, the Middle East was a cauldron of activity, where people made great advances in the arts, technology, and architecture. Societies were becoming more and more intertwined through trade networks, and relied more and more on each other for acquiring raw materials like gems, wood, ore, and grains. Societies needed these resources to survive. Elites increasingly coveted luxury goods as a way of displaying their power and wealth. As a result, leaders of small nation-states began to expand their territory into empires, empires that would wax and wane, passing from one king or monarch to another.

In about 2300 B.C., the Akkadians, under King Sargon I, built the first empire in northern Mesopotamia, which lasted about 150 years.

Later, Egyptian, Hittite, Sumer, Babylonian, Assyrian, and other empires all rose and fell. Around the eighteenth century B.C., the Code of Hammurabi, written by a Babylonian king, was etched in stone. The code, which contributed strongly to Mesopotamian civilization and evolved over a long period of time, tells us a great deal about daily life and attitudes in Babylonia.

Another ruler to emerge in the region was King David, a man who united the cities of Canaan and made Jerusalem the center of the Israeli kingdom. Israel flourished under King Solomon, who garnered for the kingdom prestige and wealth on par with Egypt and other empires. But by about 722 B.C., Israel fell to the Assyrians and the Israelites were cast out.

Some two hundred years later, the Persians under King Cyrus the Great began a new era of mega-empire in the Middle East. Beginning with the Persians, foreign armies surged into the Middle East and one by one conquered the entire region, yoking together a network of nation-states into one regional empire.

So what began as small groups of foragers settling around Israel some 12,000 years ago developed into a great surging mosaic of cultures and empires all vying for power and prestige. By the time leaders of mega-empires—for example, the Greeks and the Romans—arrived on the scene, rich cosmopolitan centers of commerce and art were thriving all across the region. Starting with the Persians and King Cyrus the Great, followed by the Greeks and Alexander the Great, the Romans, the Muslims, and the Turks, the Middle East was united under one powerful group after another until the last empire, the Ottoman, fell apart in the early 1920s.

## ERA OF EMPIRE: 550 B.C. TO 1920 A.D.

Cyrus the Great established the most extensive empire in ancient times, an empire that at its height stretched from the Greek colonies along the Mediterranean Sea, eastward to the Hindu–Kush region in present-day Afghanistan. Cyrus was Persian, a group of Indo-European horse-riding peoples from Central Asia who settled in Iran near the end of the second millennium.

## The Persians

In less than 30 years, Cyrus the Great and his leaders lifted the Persians from obscurity and established Persia as a world power. The Persians divided their empire into administrative regions, each headed by local governors and military supervisors and administrators who kept official records. The Persians allowed the regions a fair amount of local control, but royal inspectors kept a close watch. The empire was linked through an impressive system of roads, allowing their armies and couriers to reach the remotest areas in about two weeks.

The Persians revolutionized trade by creating an economy based on a silver and gold coinage system and, under their rule, trade flourished throughout the Middle East. As a result of such vibrant commercial activity, many Persian words used by traders—bazaar, shawl, sash, turquoise, tiara, orange, lemon, melon, peach, spinach, and asparagus—were adopted throughout the Middle East and eventually became part of many languages, including English. Agriculture and tribute were also large sources of revenue for the Persian Empire, an empire that reigned for about two hundred years.

## Alexander the Great and the Greeks

Alexander the Great followed the Persians. In 336 B.C. Alexander, only 20 years old, assumed the Greek throne and two years later set out to fuse the Greek and Iranian cultures into a new world empire. Within four years, Alexander the Great quickly conquered Egypt and Babylonia and drove his armies into the heart of the Persian Empire at Persepolis (southwest Iran) and burned it to the ground, proclaiming himself king over essentially the same lands the Persians had previously ruled.

Alexander married the daughter of a powerful Persian chief, and later in a mass ceremony at Susa (southwest Iran, ancient city of Elam), commanded his 10,000 soldiers to marry Iranian women in a symbolic consummation of the Greek and Iranian cultures.

But almost as quickly as he rose, death snuffed Alexander's dreams, and one year after this mass ceremony, he succumbed to a fever in Babylon at the age of 33. At its height, however, Alexander's empire was one of the first to yoke East and West together. He dominated not only all of Persia's former territories but also Greece and the Balkans in Europe. Alexander blended the Greek version of the city-state with the Persian ideas of empire and brought the East and West closer together.

## The Romans

After Alexander, Roman dominance slowly crept eastward and westward until their sphere of influence stretched from the Black Sea to the Red Sea and from the Nile to the Atlantic. Similar to the Greeks and the Persians, the Romans centered their influence in towns and cities throughout the empire; however, they ruled with a much firmer hand and a greater sense of control emanated from Rome (Fromkin et al., 2003). Like the Persians, the Romans built an extensive network of roads that wove the empire tightly together, allowing Roman administrators and travelers to efficiently move from the Gulf of Aqaba to the coasts of Spain and France.

With constant threats from the Persians and others, the Romans soon tired of maintaining their vast empire and split it in two, with Byzantium forming its eastern outpost. Byzantium is the name used for the Eastern Roman Empire in the middle ages. Roman leaders formally christened the ancient Greek city of Byzantium, located on the western tip of the Bosporus strait, as "new Rome" in 330 A.D. Later, Byzantium would be named Constantinople.

Constantinople, by virtue of its location at the crossroads between Europe and Asia, became a great trading center. Merchants exported luxury goods—wines, spices, and silk—and imported furs, fish, caviar, honey, and amber.

However, for new Rome, war or the threat of war loomed. The Romans defeated the Persians around 640 A.D., only to face a new threat from Islam and the Arabs.

Toward the end of the seventh century A.D., the Arabs made almost yearly attacks on Constantinople and by 700 A.D. new Rome teetered on ruin. Successive Roman leaders defended Byzantium from Arab and other usurpers for the next 500 years or so, but eventually the weakened empire fell.

## Arab Empire

Byzantium's final, fateful challenge came from Islam. By about 400 A.D., Christianity had become well established in most of the Roman Empire. But on the Arabian Peninsula, Islam, promoted by Muhammad bin Abdullah, born in 570 A.D. in Mecca, soon began to transform the Arab world. Muhammad, a former camel train manager, claimed God spoke to him and used him as an envoy to deliver the Koran to the Arab peoples. As Judaism and Christianity before it, Islam proclaimed monotheism. But Muhammad exhorted that—unlike earlier proclamations by Abraham, Moses, and Jesus—the messages he brought were the Lord's final words, and only those who submitted completely could understand the message. Islam in Arabic literally means "to submit." However, unlike Christianity, believers in Islam also extended the religion to encompass a system of government, law, society, and community, where all political and religious power resided within the religious community.

At first, the people of Mecca opposed Muhammad and his small group of followers and banished them to Medina. Muhammad died in 632 but Islam continued to expand. The Arabs conquered Syria in 636 and then Persia in 642. Arabs, through the imposition of a head tax, encouraged their vanquished to convert to Islam. The Arabs tolerated Christians and Jews, "people of the Book" as Arabs referred to them, but followers of these two religions were relegated to second-class citizenship.

Eventually, around 1096, Christianity and Islam clashed during the first of many Crusades. Fearing the rise of Islamic influence and the presence of Muslims in Jerusalem, Pope Urban II urged Europeans to recover the Holy Land. The pope and other religious leaders feared that Islam was gaining too much power in Christianity's birthplace and might usurp the Christian faith. Wearing the cross as an emblem of Jesus Christ's death, noblemen as well as common citizens set out to take back Jerusalem.

However, the Muslims, under a succession of leaders called caliphs, continued to expand their empire, which would eventually stretch through Spain and parts of southern France in the west, to Turkey and parts of India in the east.

From the eighth to the twelfth centuries, the Muslim world, centered in modern-day Baghdad, enjoyed great prosperity. Muslim merchants facilitated trade throughout China, Western Europe, Russia, and Africa, and a new banking system allowed checks drawn at one bank to be cashed at branches throughout the empire. Mathematicians developed the Arab *sifr*, or zero, founded algebra, and developed the Arab decimal system, which facilitated science. Muslim scientists were the first to emphasize experimentation to prove theories and develop methods for evaporation, filtration, and distillation.

Astronomers estimated the speed of light and sound, improved the astrolabe to determine the exact times the sun rose and set (which was important to Islam during Ramadan, the period of fasting from sunrise to sunset), and doctors diagnosed smallpox and measles for the first time and developed many herbal remedies. Arab pharmacists stocked camphor, cloves, myrrh, syrups, juleps, and rosewater. Herbs Arabs used in healing, like basil, oregano, and thyme, eventually found their way to European dinner tables.

Arabs borrowed the Roman horseshoe arch in their architecture and refined it for their own mosques, creating elegant and daring designs. Arabs were superb sailors and developed navigational charts and maps. An Arab pilot guided Vasco de Gama, the fifteenth-century Italian sailor who explored the eastern coast of Africa.

Meanwhile, the Turks, who began to succeed in uniting the nomads of Central Asia, as well as the Mongols, began to rival Arab dominance. In 1258, the Mongols sacked Baghdad, ending the Arab reign and setting the stage for the Ottoman Empire.

## The Ottomans

Early in the thirteenth century, the Turks controlled only a small outpost on the Anatolia Peninsula. But led by the tribe of Osman, the eventual namesake for the empire, the Ottomans gradually extended their power, and by 1345 A.D., captured all of Anatolia and fought their way into Europe, seizing most of the Balkan Peninsula.

In their quest for empire, the Ottomans used a slave system to help them rule. This system of slavery, however, was unlike slavery in the American South. The Ottoman sultans paid, clothed, and housed the slaves, later known as *janissaries*, and trained them as soldiers and administrators. The janissaries, were mostly Christian boys who converted to Islam and fought for the empire.

By 1453, the Ottomans captured Constantinople and renamed it Istanbul. The Ottomans then set their eyes on Palestine, Syria, Mesopotamia (Iraq), and Egypt, and by 1517 controlled these regions.

The Ottoman Empire experienced its Golden Age in the sixteenth century under Süleyman the Magnificent, who encouraged artists, intellectuals, craftsmen, and engineers. These visionaries excelled in the arts and law, and built many projects, including mosques, aqueducts, bridges, parks, gardens, and other public works. Under Süleyman, the Ottoman Empire was the most powerful state in the world. The extent of the empire peaked in the late 1600s, stretching from Eastern Europe to Baghdad, to parts of the Arabian Peninsula and North Africa. The Ottoman Empire, ruled from the thirteenth century to the twentieth century by the Osman dynasty, stood until the Europeans nibbled away at its borders and finally dismantled it after World War I.

Some historians and observers claim that the stability the Ottomans brought to the Middle East eroded when the empire's overarching political and economic structures were pulled apart, planting the seeds of strife, conflict, and human suffering that have ravaged the Middle East.

## CONFLICT AND STRIFE: 1920 TO 2004

At the close of World War I, Europe seemed to promise independence to the peoples of the Middle East but instead, peace brought a series of arbitrary states—Syria, Transjordan (modern Jordan), Palestine, and Iraq—carved out of the Ottoman Empire. The arbitrary boundaries drawn by Europeans cut off families and tribes from each other, and Arabs still dispute these borders. Any hope for independence after the fall of the Ottoman Empire faded after the League of Nations installed Britain and France as overseers of the countries of the Fertile Crescent.

The British installed governments in Iraq and Palestine; France imposed its rule over Syria and Lebanon. The British and French were supposed to prepare the Arabs for independence but the arrangement evolved into a new brand of colonialism.

As a result, the British and French, who had their own national and security interests to satisfy, were able to install puppet leaders, giving the impression of self-rule. Thus, after the Ottomans, most of the Middle East—excluding Turkey, Israel, and Egypt—crept forward as a collection of fragile countries ruled by foreign powers.

Throughout the twentieth century and the beginning of the twenty-first century, the Arabs of the Middle East have struggled for independence and a sense of identity. This struggle has resulted in foreign occupation, war, strife, political turmoil, economic instability, and an uneven distribution of wealth. Nowhere has that struggle been more apparent than in Palestine, home of the Arab–Israeli conflict.

## THE ARAB–ISRAELI CONFLICT

Britain first announced its support for a Jewish homeland in Palestine in 1917 in the Balfour Declaration. For the about three decades, conflict simmered between Arabs and Jews and then erupted at the end of World War II. The horrors of the Holocaust led to a renewed effort to provide a Jewish homeland and in 1947 Britain announced it was ending its mandate over Palestine. The Jews, led by their first prime minister, David Ben-Gurion, declared the state of Israel in 1948 and the Arabs immediately attacked. For a year, Israel battled Syria, Egypt, Iraq, Lebanon, and Jordan and eventually prevailed in what Israelis call their War of Independence.

Israel's War of Independence left Palestine fragmented and Egypt in control of the Gaza Strip, a small stretch of land on the Mediterranean between Israel and Egypt. After the war, Jordan annexed the West Bank, an oval-shaped swath of land that includes parts of Jerusalem and sits on the western edge of the Dead Sea between Israel and Jordan.

The war also created about 700,000 refugees when many Arabs fled the fighting. Many of the refugees or their kin remain displaced, some still living in refugee camps; the question of how to accommodate these refugees is a major issue in peace talks between the Palestinian Liberation Organization (PLO) and the Israelis. Yasir Arafat became the leader of the PLO in the 1960s and has often pushed for the right of Arabs to resettle in Palestine.

Since this initial conflict, fighting has erupted many times between the Israelis and the Arabs. In the mid-1950s, the Israelis repulsed an Egyptian attack and in 1967 during the Six-Day War prevailed again over Egypt, Syria, and Jordan. During the Six-Day War, Israel captured the Gaza Strip, parts of the Sinai Peninsula (between the Red Sea and the Mediterranean), the West Bank, all of Jerusalem—which it had only partially controlled since 1949—and the Golan Heights from Syria.

Israel still occupies all but the Sinai Peninsula and has established Jewish settlements in some of these occupied lands. Many Arabs view Israeli occupation and the many Jewish settlements as an illegitimate land grab. This friction led to the biggest clash between the Arabs and Israelis in 1974 during the Yom Kippur War, when Egypt and Syria attacked Israeli troops in the Sinai Peninsula and in the Golan Heights. The Israelis prevailed again and control over the Golan Heights, the West Bank, and the Gaza Strip remain a major issue in peace talks.

**Land for Peace**

After the 1973 Yom Kippur War, Israelis began to vigorously debate the idea of giving up portions of some of the territories it captured in return for peace, the "land for peace" compromise that is often evoked during talks between the PLO and Israel. The two sides remain bitterly divided over claims to territory.

Frustration on the part of the Arabs has led in recent years to a cycle of violence between the two sides. The violence has often been labeled as intifada, which in Arabic means "shaking off." During the intifadas of 1987 and 2000, Arabs took to the streets in protest over Israeli occupation. The protests were violent and punctuated by a string of Arab terrorist attacks, including suicide bombers who targeted Israeli civilians on buses, in temples, and in other public places. Arab youths and Arab soldiers clashed in the streets with Israeli troops. The Israelis almost always responded to the terrorist and other attacks with military strikes aimed at organizers of the Arab assaults, but sometimes the Israeli strikes also resulted in the deaths of innocent Arab civilians.

For decades, the United States, a strong ally of Israel, and other nations have tried to help broker a peace agreement between the two sides with varying degrees of success.

In 1978, Israel and Egypt made peace and Israel returned the Sinai Peninsula to Egypt. In 1993, Israeli and PLO leaders meeting secretly in Oslo, Norway, hammered out the Oslo Accords. This time, Israel officially recognized the PLO as the representative of the Palestinians and established a time line for Palestinian self-rule.

The PLO recognized Israel's right to exist and promised to abandon the use of terrorist attacks against the Jewish state. Another round of Oslo Accords two years later called for the Israelis to relinquish control of more land, the establishment of a Palestinian Council, and the election of a president of that council.

The Oslo Accords were controversial in Israel and factions disagreed on how peace with the Arabs should be accomplished. The rift in Jewish society led to many groups vying for their own visions of peace. One of the main issues Jews disagree about is whether to trade some of the land they occupy in exchange for promises from Arabs to live peacefully with the Jews, the "land for peace" compromise. In 1995, a Jewish student belonging to a fringe group that opposed giving away land for peace assassinated Prime Minister Yitzhak Rabin, leaving the country even more bitterly divided.

In 2000, peace talks between the two sides broke down again and the PLO lost perhaps its best chance in decades to gain its own state when its leaders refused to accept land-for-peace concessions from Israel that went well beyond what any other Israeli leaders had ever previously offered. Two major sticking points this time involved how to share control of Jerusalem, and the Arabs demand that all refugees and their descendants from the 1948–1949 War of Independence be allowed to return and live in Israel. The refugees numbered about three million at that time. Jewish leaders felt it would have been impossible for their country, with a population of about five million Jews and about one million Arabs, to absorb that many Palestinians and still maintain their own identity as a Jewish state.

The most recent intifada began in 2000 and at times appeared on the verge of erupting into a regional war. Both sides agreed on cease-fire resolutions only to later break them and in October 2003, the conflict spilled over the Israeli border when the Israeli military bombed suspected Palestinian terrorist training camps in Syria.

In the century of strife that has marred the Middle East since World War I, the Arab–Israeli conflict is just one piece of the puzzle. Many other conflicts, including a civil war in Lebanon, an eight-year war between Iraq and Iran, and also the Iranian revolution, have flared in the region. And though the United States has been a relative latecomer to the Middle East compared to Western Europe, it has made up for lost time by waging two wars in the region since 1993.

## THE GULF WARS

The first war in Iraq ("Desert Storm") came in 1991 on the heels of Hussein's attempt to annex Kuwait, a neighboring country to the south of Iraq on the Persian Gulf. Iraq and Kuwait have long disputed their common border, and many Iraqis have always considered Kuwait and its rich oil fields to be part of Iraq. In 1990, on the heels of fighting a war with Iran from 1980–1988, Iraq found itself nearly bankrupt. In an attempt to bolster his country's finances, Saddam Hussein attacked Kuwait and took over the Kuwaiti oil fields.

A broad coalition of governments led by the United States quickly liberated Kuwait from the invading Iraqi army but Hussein remained in power.

In the years following the first Gulf War, many believed Hussein built up a stockpile of lethal weapons, including chemical, biological, and perhaps even nuclear. Hussein had previously used chemical weapons on his own people and also used them during the Iran–Iraq War, so it was a widely held assumption he might use the weapons again. Then, in the wake of the September 11, 2001 terrorist attacks, many American leaders feared Hussein might provide his weapons of mass destruction to terrorists bent on using these weapons to attack cities in the United States.

Although many countries and the United Nations disagreed with the United States as to whether Hussein actually harbored weapons of mass destruction, the United States, Britain, and other coalition countries attacked Iraq in February 2003 with the intent of toppling Hussein and seizing the weapons before they fell into the hands of terrorists. More than one year later, American and British troops had failed to find the arsenal of weapons they claimed Hussein was hiding.

In December 2003, American troops captured Hussein and by that time almost 500 American soldiers had died fighting in Iraq. President Bush declared the end of major combat operations in May but attacks against coalition forces continued. More Americans were killed after May than during the main combat operations, which began in March, and many thought Hussein was directing the attacks. By May, the death toll stood at 800. Yet the attacks continued almost unabated even after American troops captured Hussein, leading many to think the insurgency was more organic than originally believed. It appeared to many observers that the insurgents were acting on their own and not out of an allegiance with Hussein.

If so, what were they fighting for? Some have argued the insurgents' zeal to carry on the fight can be traced back to Iraq's experiences with Western domination since the end of World War I, when Britain in effect colonized the country. The memory of British occupation was fresh in the insurgents' minds and they rejected the U.S. and British presence in their country in the new millennium. Although President Bush said the forces were there to liberate Iraq, increasingly the Iraqi insurgents saw U.S. troops as an occupation force.

Charges that the U.S. military and other coalition forces abused and murdered detainees at the Abu Gharib prison in Iraq and prisons in Afghanistan threatened to undermine U.S. credibility. The U.S. promised to hand Iraq over to an interim Iraqi government by June 30, but with the increasing violence some questioned if the U.S. could meet the commitment.

The insurgents' actions must also be viewed through the lens of Middle East history, which as we have seen, has been greatly influenced by clashes between Eastern and Western powers—for example, the Crusades beginning in the eleventh century. Furthermore, these clashes have often been rooted in religious differences—Islam versus Christianity—a clash that has manifested a form of Islamic militancy known today as Islamic fundamentalism, which we will discuss later.

## Why Was the United States Willing to Wage Two Wars in Iraq?

Toppling Hussein was important to protect U.S. access to the region's oil reserves and also, as Bush and others argued, to liberate the

Iraqi people and help secure the United States from threats of terrorism. The United States relies heavily on access to Middle Eastern oil, importing millions of barrels annually. If events in the Middle East cut off access to these reserves, the ensuing rise in gasoline prices could cripple the American economy, lead to inflation, high unemployment, and other long-term problems.

As September 11 proved, terrorism is a major problem in the world, not only for the United States but also for many countries around the world, including the Middle East. Many Middle Eastern governments face the same fears of terrorism as the United States and have been attacked by the same extremists. These attacks stem from the growing influence of Islamic fundamentalism that plagues the Middle East.

## ISLAMIC FUNDAMENTALISM

The rise of Islamic fundamentalism challenges nearly every government in the Middle East and has been the source of much strife in the region as well as terrorism around the world. The surge of Islamic fundamentalism is one of the most important challenges facing the Middle East. Leaders of this movement reject Western influences, values, and secular society as decadent and destructive to Muslims. These extremists want their governments to enforce Islamic law, or Sharia, a form of rule where all aspects of life and nation are governed based on strict interpretations of the Koran.

This movement began in the waning years of the Ottoman Empire and picked up momentum in the first part of the twentieth century as the Middle East shed colonial rule and began searching for its own sense of identity. Proponents of Islamic fundamentalism believe Muslims must revert to their Islamic heritage in order to combat Western influence, which requires overthrowing all non-Islamic societies. It must be noted, however, that Islamic fundamentalists, especially those who endorse violence, make up a very small minority of the population in the Middle East. In addition, although these militants espouse the Koran in their calls for jihad—which they define as "holy war"—their definition of jihad is based on their own interpretation of the Koran, which varies from mainstream Islamic society. The Koran does not proscribe a political connotation to the term *jihad*. Literally, jihad in the Koran calls for the struggle to right a wrong or to protect oneself against an aggressor, and on a more psychological level, the internal struggle to be a better Muslim.

## The Iranian Revolution

Islamic fundamentalism sparked the Iranian revolution in 1979 and later led to the eight-year war between Iran and Iraq because Saddam Hussein feared the Shiite Muslims in his country would seek to revolt along with Shiite revolutionaries in Iran.

Ayatollah Khomeini, living abroad, led Islamic fundamentalists in Iran, who overthrew a Western-backed monarchy. The revolutionaries saw the Iranian monarchy as corrupt and repressive, yet even after the revolution, many Iranians also questioned Islamic clerics whom they saw as equally corrupt and unable to provide the social justice they sought. Some young Iranians have rioted and protested in recent years and are more pro-Western than many of their Middle Eastern peers. Many Iranians felt Islamic law improved some things but criticized the clerics as unwilling to create more democratic, free, and secular societies (Fromkin et al., 2003).

## Islamic Fundamentalism and Terrorism

Others in the Middle East, inspired by the Iranian revolution, began to seek Islamic rule in their own countries and lashed out at leaders viewed as "oppressive." In 1979, Muslim militants seized the Grand Mosque in Mecca as a sign of protest against Saudi Arabian leadership. In 1981, Muslim militants assassinated Egyptian president Anwar Sadat. In 1984, Hezbollah (Islamic militants aligned with the Shiite sect in Iran) drove a car bomb into the U.S. embassy and military barracks in Lebanon and killed dozens, forcing the United States out of Lebanon.

In the 1990s, Hamas, Islamic Jihad, and other Islamic groups resorted to violence in an effort to thwart Arab–Israeli peace plans. Despite the PLO's recognition of the right of Israel to exist, these groups sought to destroy the state of Israel and chase all Jews from Palestine.

The menace of Islamic fundamentalism remains fresh in the minds of Americans who suffered attacks by these groups. Islamic fundamentalists led by Osama bin Laden flew passenger jets into the World Trade Center and the Pentagon and crashed another jet in a field in Pennsylvania, killing and injuring thousands. The threat of more attacks spurred America to launch a war on terrorism around the world and to undertake its most recent war in Iraq.

Islamic fundamentalism is perhaps one of the biggest challenges faced by nearly every government in the Middle East. The major dilemma for most countries is how to best maintain Islamic heritage and traditions in a modern, global world that offers many alternatives or variations to an Islamic lifestyle. As we shall see, slow economic growth in the Middle East has fueled the rise of Islamic fundamentalism. Many young people, frustrated by high unemployment and ill equipped to compete in the global marketplace, have turned to Islamic fundamentalism as a way to bolster their own sense of identity and self-worth.

## STUDY QUESTIONS

1. Where is the Fertile Crescent and why is it called the cradle of civilization? How did domestication of plants and animals help spawn the world's first urban centers? Approximately when did civilization take hold?
2. Domestication of plants and animals are examples of technology. What other examples of technology did early civilizations create? How did these examples of technology help establish urban centers?
3. Name some of the earliest empires in the Middle East. Why did the leaders of the Sumerians and others desire to build empires?
4. Name some of the mega-empires that ruled over the entire Middle East. How do these empires still impact the modern Middle East?
5. What are some of the artistic, religious, and scientific contributions of the Arabs?
6. Who are the Ottomans and when did they reign? What are some Ottoman contributions that still impact modern times?
7. What is the so-called land-for-peace compromise? Do you agree with it?
8. Why is peace and prosperity in the Middle East so important to U.S. interests? To the world as a whole?
9. What is Islamic fundamentalism? How has this movement impacted the Middle East?

# CHAPTER 4

# Economics

The Middle East is hobbled by high unemployment, lack of personal freedom, and poor educational systems. These factors—coupled with the turmoil in the Gaza Strip, the West Bank, Israel, and Iraq, terrorists bombings and assassinations, and squabbles over borders—have created a specter of instability that hovers over the region. This instability has led to a growing sense of uncertainty among those living in the Middle East and fomented a sense of frustration and resignation. After the events of September 11, 2001, this sense of fear and instability has reverberated even louder.

This instability and the fear it engenders is a major challenge that inhibits growth and development in the Middle East. In order to shake off the malaise that has settled in the region, the people need peace and security but even that alone won't be enough. Many Middle Eastern economists in the 2002 United Nations Human Development Report also stated that the Middle East must improve education, equity between men and women, and basic human rights, such as a free flow of information and democratic and transparent government, in order to foster a stronger economy.

## THE COST OF UNREST

Unrest is expensive in many ways. Due to constant conflict, Middle Eastern countries spend enormous amounts of money building and maintaining large armies. As a percentage of their total revenues, Middle Eastern countries spend more on their militaries than all other countries in the world. This is money that could be spent more wisely on improving education and building schools and hospitals, which some Middle East countries need. Wars destroy roads, buildings, and bridges, lead to inflation, and tear at a country's psychological and social foundations.

In addition, all countries need foreign investment to prosper. However, people prefer to invest their money in stable countries with open, transparent governments and where corruption is limited. If a region is unstable, investors go elsewhere. Also, most companies prefer to do business with governments that operate transparently and have little corruption. A government is transparent if its decision-making process is open and easily observable by the general public. Democracy is a form of transparent government.

However, most governments in the Middle East are centralized and controlled by one ruler. Of all the countries in the region, only the peoples of Israel and Turkey live in democracies. Dictators, kings, monarchs, and tribal leaders rule over the rest of the Middle East. When a government is not transparent, it's easier for corrupt officials to bribe businessmen, which raises the cost of doing business.

## THE "FREEDOM DEFICIT"

The lack of democracy and personal freedom in the Middle East directly affects the economy. The wave of democracy that transformed governments around the world in the 1980s and early 1990s barely touched the Middle East. While Latin America, East Asia, Eastern Europe, and other regions were democratizing, the Middle East pursued various forms of one-man or centralized rule. Many Middle East countries enshrine democracy and human rights in their constitutions but it's primarily lip service. In reality, these promises, like the right to vote and equality between men and women, are denied to most people in this region. Some countries have "elections," but only one candidate is placed on the ballot and opposition parties are restricted. In theory, many countries also have democratic institutions, like legislatures and executive and judicial branches of government, but in reality, the institutions have little power. Israel is the truest democracy in the region, using a parliamentary style form of rule. Turkey is the only other democratic government in the Middle East; however, the Turkish military is an 800-pound gorilla that exerts much influence, often limiting what the Turkish government can do. This "freedom deficit," as some economists call it, undermines development and limits political development.

## THE COST OF POOR EDUCATION

Poor education is another hindrance to the economy in this region. In 2003, nearly 65 million adult Arabs were illiterate, with two-thirds of them being women. Since the fall of the Ottoman Empire, educational systems in most Middle East countries have been rooted in Islamic traditions and literature and have tended to emphasize preparation for the professions or government service, ignoring the technical and vocational training needed to produce skilled workers who can compete in a globalized world. Globalization emphasizes mastering computers and other technology in order to compete for jobs and industry. However, the Middle Eastern education systems tend to foster a mismatch between what students learn and what the labor market demands. Less than one percent of the population in the Middle East uses the Internet and a little more than one percent uses personal computers.

## THE MIDDLE EAST'S BURGEONING YOUTH

Another challenge to development and to educating young Middle Easterners is the growing number of young people. Children under 14 account for 40 percent of the total population in Arab countries, with people over 60 making up only about 5 percent (Regional Bureau for Arab States 2002). Comparatively, the United States has about half as many children under 14 and about three times as many people over 60. Compounding this problem is a high birth rate in most Middle Eastern countries, a rate that exceeds the global average. Women in some countries, like Bahrain and Lebanon, have about 2.2 babies in their lifetime; however, in Yemen, women average 7.6 births (Regional Bureau for Arab States 2002).

These large numbers of young people often outstrip many Middle Eastern countries' abilities to provide classrooms and educational resources for children. Ten million children in the Middle East between the ages of 6 and 15 years do not attend school (Regional Bureau for Arab States 2002).

## BIG OIL

Another important aspect of the Middle Eastern economy is oil. Arabs first discovered oil under Middle Eastern sands around the turn of the twentieth century, but did not turn it into a major industry until about the 1950s. The Middle East discovered it had what the world wanted and in the 1960s, leaders of Saudi Arabia, Kuwait, Iraq, Iran, and also Venezuela, formed OPEC (the Organization of Petroleum Exporting Countries) and used oil to improve their economic bargaining power. OPEC sets quotas for production as a way to control the worldwide price of oil.

Oil allowed many countries to modernize and build schools, hospitals, roads, and government buildings. It brought great wealth to some and allowed leaders of oil-rich countries to maintain their power and influence. However, oil also widened an ever-increasing gap between the rich and poor in the Middle East. Saudi Arabians, for example, do not pay taxes, and oil revenues pay for many social services and help to stimulate household income. At the height of the old boom in 1974, Saudi per capita income was $6,991, while Jordanians earned $428, Syrians made $340, and Egyptians a mere $240 (Fromkin et al., 2003). The income gap in the Middle East is still quite large (see GDP per capita later in this chapter).

Arab reliance on oil, however, has hindered diversification of the Middle East economy. The oil-producing countries rely heavily on this single industry, and few Middle East countries have diverse economies.

## SIGNS OF IMPROVEMENT

Although many problems plague the Middle East, the region has improved its literacy rates and lowered birth rates; incomes for some have grown dramatically. As the region improves, expectations and aspirations for democracy and freedom have grown and basic living standards have risen. However, many countries have been unable to meet their people's expectations. Middle Eastern leaders will have to meet these challenges in a way that fits with the history and traditions in their countries, which means satisfying the desires stirred by nationalism.

**Table 4.1.    Oil Reserves**

*World Reserves (in billions of barrels)*

| | |
|---|---|
| Middle East | 724 |
| South America | 92 |
| Remainder of the world | 82 |
| Europe and Soviet Union | 76 |
| North America | 58 |
| **Total World Reserves** | **1,032** |

*Middle East Oil Reserves (in billions of barrels)*

| | |
|---|---|
| Saudi Arabia | 259 |
| Iraq | 113 |
| United Arab Emirates | 98 |
| Kuwait | 94 |
| Iran | 90 |
| Libya | 30 |
| Qatar | 15 |
| Algeria | 9 |
| Oman | 6 |
| Egypt | 3 |
| Other Middle East countries | 7 |

## FACTS AND FIGURES: PEOPLE

### *Algeria*

**Population:** 32,818,500
**Ethnic groups:** Arab-Berber 99%; European less than 1%
**Religion:** Sunni Muslim (state religion) 99%, Christian and Jewish 1%
**Literacy:** total 70%, men 79%, women 61%
**Median age:** 22.5 years
**GDP per capita:** $5,300

### *Bahrain*

**Population:** 667,238; *Note*: includes 235,108 non-nationals (July 2003 *estimate*)
**Ethnic groups:** Bahraini 63%, Asian 19%, other Arab 10%, Iranian 8%
**Religion:** Shiite Muslim 70%, Sunni Muslim 30%
**Literacy:** total 89%, men 92%, women 85%
**Median age:** 29
**GDP per capita:** $14,000

## Egypt

**Population:** 74,718,797

**Ethnic groups:** Eastern Hamitic stock (Egyptians, Bedouins, and Berbers) 99%, Greek, Nubian, Armenian, other European (primarily Italian and French) 1%

**Religion:** Muslim (mostly Sunni) 94%, Coptic Christian and other 6%

**Literacy:** total 58%, men 68%, women 47%

**Median age:** 23

**GDP per capita:** $3,900

## Iran

**Population:** 68,278,826

**Ethnic groups:** Persian 51%, Azeri 24%, Gilaki and Mazandarani 8%, Kurd 7%, Arab 3%, Lur 2%, Baloch 2%, Turkmen 2%, other 1%

**Religion:** Shiite Muslim 89%, Sunni Muslim 10%, Zoroastrian, Jewish, Christian, and Baha'i 1%

**Literacy:** total 79%, men 86%, women 73%

**Median age:** 23

**GDP per capita:** $7,000

## Iraq

**Population:** 24,683,313

**Ethnic groups:** Arab 75%–80%, Kurdish 15%–20%, Turkoman, Assyrian or other 5%

**Religion:** Muslim 97% (Shiite 60%–65%, Sunni 32%–37%), Christian or other 3%

**Literacy:** total 40%, men 56%, women 24%

**Median age:** 19

**GDP per capita:** $2,400

## Israel

**Population:** 6,116,533; *Note:* includes about 187,000 Israeli settlers in the West Bank, about 20,000 in the Israeli-occupied Golan Heights, more than 5,000 in the Gaza Strip, and fewer than 177,000 in East Jerusalem

**Ethnic groups:** Jewish 80.1% (Europe/America-born 32.1%, Israel-born 20.8%, Africa-born 14.6%, Asia-born 12.6%), non-Jewish 19.9% (mostly Arab)

**Religion:** Jewish 80.1%, Muslim 14.6% (mostly Sunni Muslim), Christian 2.1%, other 3.2%

**Literacy:** total 95%, men 97%, women 94%

**Median age:** 29

**GDP per capita:** $19,000

## Jordan

**Population:** 5,460,265

**Ethnic groups:** Arab 98%, Circassian 1%, Armenian 1%

**Religion:** Sunni Muslim 92%, Christian 6% (majority Greek Orthodox, but some Greek and Roman Catholics, Syrian Orthodox, Coptic Orthodox, Armenian Orthodox, and Protestant denominations), other 2% (several small Shiite Muslim and Druze populations)

**Literacy:** total 91%, men 96%, women 86%

**Median age:** 22

**GDP per capita:** $4,300

## Kuwait

**Population:** 2,183,161; *Note:* includes 1,291,354 non-nationals

**Ethnic groups:** Kuwaiti 45%, other Arab 35%, South Asian 9%, Iranian 4%, other 7%

**Religion:** Muslim 85% (Sunni 70%, Shiite 30%), Christian, Hindu, Parsi, and other 15%

**Literacy:** total 84%, men 85%, women 82%

**Median age:** 26

**GDP per capita:** $15,000

## Lebanon

**Population:** 3,727,703

**Ethnic groups:** Arab 95%, Armenian 4%, other 1%

**Religion:** Muslim 70% (including Shiite, Sunni, Druze, Isma'ilite, Alawite or Nusayri), Christian 29% (including Orthodox Christian, Catholic, Protestant), Jewish, less than 1%
**Literacy:** total 87%, men 93%, women 82%
**Median age:** 26
**GDP per capita:** $5,400

## Libya

**Population:** 5,499,074; *Note:* includes 166,510 non-nationals
**Ethnic groups:** Berber and Arab 97%, Greeks, Maltese, Italians, Egyptians, Pakistanis, Turks, Indians, Tunisians 3%
**Religion:** Sunni Muslim 97%
**Literacy:** total 83%, men 92%, women 72%
**Median age:** 23
**GDP per capita:** $7,600

## Morocco

**Population:** 31,689,265
**Ethnic groups:** Arab-Berber 99.1%, other 0.7%, Jewish 0.2%
**Religion:** Muslim 98.7%, Christian 1.1%, Jewish 0.2%
**Literacy:** total 52%, men 64%, women 39%
**Median age:** 23
**GDP per capita:** $3,900

## Oman

**Population:** 2,807,125; *Note:* includes 577,293 non-nationals
**Ethnic groups:** Arab, Baluchi, South Asian (Indian, Pakistani, Sri Lankan, Bangladeshi), African
**Religion:** Ibadhi Muslim 75%, Sunni Muslim, Shiite Muslim, Hindu 25%
**Literacy:** total 76%, men 83%, women 67%
**Median age:** 19
**GDP per capita:** $8,300

## *Palestine (Gaza Strip)*

**Population:** 1,274,868; *Note:* in addition, there are more than 5,000 Israeli settlers in the Gaza Strip
**Ethnic groups:** Palestinian Arab and other 99.4%, Jewish 0.6%
**Religion:** Muslim (predominantly Sunni) 98.7%, Christian 0.7%, Jewish 0.6%
**Literacy:** Not available
**Median age:** 15
**GDP per capita:** $600

## *Palestine (West Bank)*

**Population:** 2,237,194; *Note:* in addition, there are about 187,000 Israeli settlers in the West Bank and fewer than 177,000 in East Jerusalem
**Ethnic groups:** Palestinian Arab and other 83%, Jewish 17%
**Religion:** Muslim 75% (predominantly Sunni), Jewish 17%, Christian and other 8%
**Literacy:** Not available
**Median age:** 18
**GDP per capita:** $800

## *Qatar*

**Population:** 817,052
**Ethnic groups:** Arab 40%, Pakistani 18%, Indian 18%, Iranian 10%, other 14%
**Religion:** Muslim 95%, other 5%
**Literacy:** total 83%, men 81%, women 85%
**Median age:** 31
**GDP per capita:** $21,500

## *Saudi Arabia*

**Population:** 24,293,844; *Note:* includes 5,576,076 non-nationals
**Ethnic groups:** Arab 90%, Afro-Asian 10%

**Religion:** Muslim 100%
**Literacy:** total 79%, men 85%, women 71%
**Median age:** 19
**GDP per capita:** $10,500

## *Syria*

**Population:** 17,585,540; *Note:* in addition, about 40,000 people live in the Israeli-occupied Golan Heights—20,000 Arabs (18,000 Druze and 2,000 Alawites) and about 20,000 Israeli settlers
**Ethnic groups:** Arab 90.3%, Kurds, Armenians, and other 9.7%
**Religion:** Sunni Muslim 74%, Alawite, Druze, and other Muslim sects 16%, Christian (various sects) 10%, Jewish (tiny communities in Damascus, Al Qamishli, and Aleppo)
**Literacy:** total 77%, men 90%, women 64%
**Median age:** 20
**GDP per capita:** $3,500

## *Tunisia*

**Population:** 9,924,742
**Ethnic groups:** Arab 98%, European 1%, Jewish and other 1%
**Religion:** Muslim 98%, Christian 1%, Jewish and other 1%
**Literacy:** total 74%, men 84%, women 64%
**Median age:** 26
**GDP per capita:** $6,500

## *Turkey*

**Population:** 68,109,469
**Ethnic groups:** Turkish 80%, Kurdish 20%
**Religion:** Muslim 99.8% (mostly Sunni), other 0.2% (mostly Christians and Jews)
**Literacy:** total 87%, men 94%, women 79%
**Median age:** 27
**GDP per capita:** $7,000

## United Arab Emirates

**Population:** 2,484,818; *Note:* includes an estimated 1,606,079 non-nationals; the 17 December 1995 census presents a total population figure of 2,377,453, and there are estimates of 3.44 million for 2002

**Ethnic groups:** Emirati 19%, other Arab and Iranian 23%, South Asian 50%, other expatriates (includes Westerners and East Asians) 8%; *Note:* less than 20% are UAE citizens

**Religion:** Muslim 96% (Shiite 16%), Christian, Hindu, and other 4%

**Literacy:** total 78%, men 76%, women 82%

**Median age:** 28

**GDP per capita:** $22,000

## Yemen

**Population:** 19,349,881

**Ethnic groups:** predominantly Arab; but also Afro-Arab, South Asians, Europeans

**Religion:** Muslim including Shaf'i (Sunni) and Zaydi (Shiite), small numbers of Jewish, Christian, and Hindu

**Literacy:** total 50%, men 71%, women 30%

**Median age:** 16

**GDP per capita:** $840

## United States

**Population:** 290,342,554

**Ethnic groups:** white 77.1%, black 12.9%, Asian 4.2%, Amerindian and Alaska native 1.5%, native Hawaiian and other Pacific islander 0.3%, other 4% (2000); *Note:* a separate listing for Hispanic is not included because the U.S. Census Bureau considers Hispanic to mean a person of Latin American descent (including persons of Cuban, Mexican, or Puerto Rican origin) living in the United States who may be of any race or ethnic group (white, black, Asian, etc.)

**Religion:** Protestant 56%, Roman Catholic 28%, Jewish 2%, other 4%, none 10% (1989)

**Literacy:** total 97%, men 97%, women 97%
**Median age:** 36
**GDP per capita:** $37,600

Source: *CIA World Factbook*, 2003
Note: Literacy refers to age 15 and over; GDP per capita represents individual purchasing power

## STUDY QUESTIONS

1. How does stability and transparency affect the Middle East economy?
2. What is secularism?
3. What countries in the Middle East have democratic governments?
4. How does the Middle East's young population impact the region?
5. How has the discovery of oil impacted the Middle East? Do all Middle East countries share equally in the wealth that oil has brought? How does access to Middle East oil impact U.S. security?
6. As far as technological innovation, how does ancient and modern Middle East compare? Do you think the Middle East, in relation to other regions of the world, was more technologically advanced during ancient/premodern times or in modern times?
7. Pick a few countries in the Middle East and compare illiteracy rates between men and women. How do they differ? What do you think are some of the reasons for the disparity in literacy rates between men and women?
8. What is the "freedom deficit" and how does this impact the Middle East?

# CHAPTER 5

# Issues of Identity

## ARAB NATIONALISM

In general, nationalism is a search for group belonging based on a national consciousness and a shared culture that is itself often based on history, traditions, and language. During a long history of dominance by foreign empires and powers, the Middle East as a whole never really achieved this sense of shared consciousness, and the same is true for most individual countries in the region.

As we've seen, the term the "Middle East" was first used about 100 years ago by Europeans to describe a region situated between Europe and the Far East. We've also learned that, beginning with Alexander the Great in about 330 B.C., the Middle East was a region stitched together by invading armies, and over the centuries this vast region and its diverse peoples were passed around from one foreign empire to another.

From Alexander the Great through the reign of the Ottoman Empire in the early twentieth century, Arabs have had little in common with the invaders who conquered them and have never developed a sense of identity with these invaders, nor have they developed a sense of identity based on territory. For example, Arabs never thought of themselves as Saudi Arabian or Egyptian, though over time, they have developed a shared sense of identity based on language, family, and tribal ties.

After World War I, Europeans forced Arabs to live in states and within borders that Europeans arbitrarily drew based on their own imperial aspirations. The new borders had little historical meaning for the

Arabs living there. As we've learned, the Europeans installed hand-picked leaders to govern these newly established states. These fragile regimes struggled to build strong states mirrored on Western ideals of statehood, and many Arabs living under these regimes resented European dominance. The one thing that united Arabs was the idea that independence was the best way to solve all the problems that plagued their new states.

With the growing desire for independence beginning early in the twentieth century, nationalist aspirations began to grow. Two major forms of nationalism emerged in the Middle East around this time. One, Pan-Arabism, sought to build a giant nation-state uniting all Arabs on the basis of their shared Arab language. The other form sought to build identities based on individual Arabic-speaking countries. Efforts to unite all Arab peoples into one giant nation, however, never took root, and a nationalism based more on a localized sense of identity, one based on states, has prevailed.

### Achieving Independence

After World War II, Iraq, Syria, Saudi Arabia, Lebanon, Jordan, and Egypt were the first Middle East states to achieve independence. Since the 1970s, all Middle Eastern countries have been self-governed. However, these fledgling states quickly learned that throwing off the yoke of colonialism was not the cure-all they envisioned. Economic stagnation, exploding populations, and rapid change continued to pose major problems. No longer able to blame their ills on European domination, many Arabs began to search for an identity to help rally their countrymen.

One of the major rallying cries for nationalists is Islam. A sense of identity based on Islam is not new in the Middle East, for as we've seen, from about the seventh to the thirteenth centuries, Muhammad and his army of followers united a vast empire based on this religion. Islam resonates among Arabs who long for a new sense of direction and accomplishment. Some Arabs, however, have tried to militarize this Islamic movement and have assassinated or sought to overthrow leaders seen as oppressors, just as the Iranians did when they swept the Muhammad Reza Shah off the throne of Iran.

### What Type of Islam Will Prevail?

Arabs have struggled to establish a brand of Islam compatible with their national aspirations. Some fundamentalists believe Islamic law, or Sharia, should govern every aspect of life and nation and believe that the *ulama*, the learned clerics, should control government. Others believe Islam should be used to guide society and adapted to a modern world. In this sense, many Arabs believe more separation of church and state is needed.

The wrenching social, psychological, economic, and political problems that arose after the fall of the Ottoman Empire continue to plague the Middle East, and it is too early to know what brand of Islam might prevail. The Arab search for identity continues, and Islamic fundamentalists, though few in number, greatly influence this search. In order to counter this virulent force, Arab politicians will likely have to make serious improvements in the economy and offer more democratic freedoms.

## RELIGION

Religion is another major aspect of identity and nowhere is this truer than in the Middle East, the birthplace of the three great monotheistic religions—Judaism, Christianity, and Islam.

### Judaism

Judaism is the saga of a people and the story began about 5,000 years ago. The road to group identity began when God summoned Abraham and his wife, Sarah, to lead a small group of nomadic peoples to settle in Canaan (modern-day Israel). The journey to group identity was a long one, with famine and slavery presenting major challenges to the people who would eventually called themselves Jews. After a series of miracles, the Jews migrated from Egypt and escaped slavery around 1250 B.C. and for the first time began to see themselves as a distinct people.

Later, God revealed himself at Mount Sinai and offered the Jews the Torah, the first five books of the Hebrew Bible. God's revelations solidified in the Jews a sense of collective identity. At Mount Sinai,

God imparted a spiritual mission upon the Jews to fulfill his will and to return to the Holy Land and form the Jewish nation of Israel, according to the Bible.

Some 300 years after the Jews returned to Israel, King Solomon built a house for God in the form of the Jerusalem Temple at Temple Mount and proclaimed all of Israel as sacred ground. The Western Wall, pockmarked by bullet and mortar fire, stands as the Temple Mount's only remaining remnant, hallowed ground "from which the Divine Presence never moves," and where Jews press close to the massive stones and pray.

Around 722 B.C., the Jews were expelled from the Holy Land. In 586 B.C., the Babylonians destroyed the Jerusalem Temple and exiled Jewish leaders, who returned 70 years later and rebuilt the temple.

Six hundred years after rebuilding, the Romans destroyed the second temple, and in 135 B.C., the final Jewish revolt ended in mass slaughter, with the surviving Jews forced again to leave Israel. Though some Jews remained in the Holy Land and others established a presence beginning in the 1920s during the Zionist movement, the majority of Jews did not return until the founding of Israel in 1948.

*What Is Judaism?*

Judaism is a specific faith for a specific people. Jews come from many races and ethnicities and although the faith allows people to convert to Judaism, unlike Christianity and Islam, it does not aspire to save or convert the world. Most Jews define members of the "tribe" or faith as those born to Jewish mothers.

Judaism was the first religion to profess monotheism, or a belief that there is only one God. Judaism was also the first religion to introduce the concept of a messiah, someone who would appear before man and bring world peace.

The Jewish Sabbath was also a revolutionary idea in the ancient world. Some Jews see this weekly observance as a way to be closer to God and to reflect. The Sabbath is a reprieve from the weight of life in the modern world. Some Jews refrain from travel, commerce, and the use of machines and electricity on the Sabbath, and through these sacrifices, Jews symbolically escape the pressures of modernity and live closer to God.

Judaism teaches its followers to not just study the Torah but also to ponder it, question it. This exploration of the story of being Jewish is central to the basic tenets of Judaism, along with service to one God. Observing Sabbath and professing allegiance to one God are ways Jews maintain a personal relationship with God, but another basic tenet of Judaism is performing acts of kindness or good deeds for others. Jews teach that good deeds help make other persons' lives better, holier, and that Jews should not expect anything in return for their acts of kindness.

Another central element of Judaism has always been a belief in the promise of a return to the Holy Land. At times, Jews saw their banishment from the Holy Land as a sign that God was punishing them for not fulfilling his will. All the while, however, Jews sustained themselves with the belief that they would return to Israel and do the Lord's bidding. Other faiths cherish the Holy Land, but Jews tie their identity to this land.

*A Diverse, Secular Israel*

The ingathering, the return of exiles to Israel from around the world, has brought together Jews from as many as a hundred countries. About six million people live in Israel and about 80 percent are Jews. Israel is a very diverse state with several groups promoting their own definitions of Judaism and their visions for the Holy Land's future. Israel is a parliamentary-style democracy and although religion plays a major role in government and in society, it is a secular state. Politicians in Israel face the constant challenge of balancing the demands of religion and state, but separating the two completely is difficult for a nation whose identity was built, in part, on religious foundations. Like many nations, Israel continues its search for identity, a search challenged by the pressures of modernity and globalization.

## Christianity

If the story of Judaism is the saga of a people, then the story of Christianity is the saga of a man, Jesus Christ. Hailing from Nazareth and born into a family of poor carpenters, Jesus lived under the Roman Empire.

The four gospels of the New Testament—Matthew, Mark, Luke, and John—tell Jesus' story, a story that is familiar to millions of people around the world. Christians believe Jesus' birth fulfilled the Jewish prophecies, which claimed a messiah would return to Earth and deliver the Jews from captivity.

Jesus was a Jew, and Christianity, along with Islam, is one of two monotheistic religions that evolved out of Judaism. Whereas Judaism centers on the Jewish people's relationship with God and the Jewish people's mission to bringing universal justice and God's will to Earth, Christianity centers on Jesus' resurrection and the belief that everyone has the right to a relationship with God, and that God forgave all mankind through Jesus' death.

Jesus began his ministry at the age of 30 and spent three years wandering, spreading his beliefs, and performing miracles. He taught through parables, stories of everyday life infused with divine messages, and proclaimed he spoke with God's authority.

During his lifetime, Jesus elaborated a heavenly vision for all mankind, including the poor and the powerless. "Blessed are the poor in spirit, for theirs is the kingdom of heaven. Blessed are the meek, for they shall inherit the earth. Blessed are those who hunger and thirst for righteousness, for they shall be satisfied," Jesus said.

*Jesus, a Revolutionary, and His Legacy*

Jesus spoke of justice for all; however, the Romans and religious authorities in Palestine perceived Jesus as a radical, a revolutionary, and convicted him of heresy, then nailed him to a cross to die with two common thieves. On the Sunday following the execution, Christians believe Jesus rose from the dead, marking a turning point for all of Western civilization.

Later, Paul, one of Jesus' missionaries, began to spread the word of Jesus' life, death, and teachings. Paul taught mankind to live in the "Holy Spirit" and that God achieved his power and influence by working through people. He also taught that a relationship with God set everyone free, not just Jews.

Paul established churches throughout the Middle East, Europe, and Africa. However, the church remained small and its followers persecuted until Constantine, a Roman soldier, proclaimed Christianity as the empire's official religion around 325 A.D.

Though Christianity spread widely, it has almost always attracted a minority of followers in the Holy Land. Only for a brief time under the Byzantine Empire in the fifth and sixth centuries did Christians make up a majority of the population in the Holy Land. With the rise of Islam in the seventh century, Muslims quickly exceeded the Christian population. Christianity maintained a solid presence for several centuries but then declined rapidly. In 1033, European Christians migrated to the Holy Land to mark the 1000th anniversary of Jesus' death, a migration that eventually spawned waves of Crusades to reestablish Christianity in the Holy Land. About the same time, a great schism divided the Christian church, leading to a split between Eastern (Constantinople) and Western (Rome) Christianity. The split, a theological disagreement over the Trinity (Father, Son, and Holy Ghost), led to the establishment of the Orthodox and Roman Catholic churches.

About 5 percent of the people living in the Middle East in 2003 called themselves Christian. The largest numbers of Christians live in Lebanon and Egypt, about 11 million and 4 million, respectively. Syria, Jordan, Iraq, and Kuwait have sizeable Christian populations as well. Small numbers of Christians live in many other Middle East countries, including Israel, whose population is about 2 percent Christian.

During the Ottoman Empire, Christians, Jews, and Muslims lived together relatively peacefully. However, European occupation of the Middle East after World War I, when Western powers allied with the Middle East Christians, strained relations among the three religions. Jewish and Muslim suffering under the Roman Empire, the legacy of the Crusades, and the Holocaust continue to resonate in the Middle East and fuel bitterness as well as the cycle of violence in the region.

### Islam

Much like Christianity, Islam centers around the life of a single man, the Prophet Muhammad, born in Mecca five hundred seventy years after Christ. Islam is based on the belief that God spoke directly to Muhammad and chose him as his messenger. Just as Moses and Christ had claimed hundreds of years earlier, Muhammad professed that God spoke to him. Over many years, Muhammad committed the words to memory and imparted them to scribes verbatim as God had spoken the words to him. Eventually, the revelations were gathered together in a single work, the Koran, the equivalent of the Jewish and Christian bibles.

### Muhammad's Special Relationship with God

For Muslims, the Koran cemented a special relationship between Muhammad and God, a relationship not found in Judaism or Christianity, which distinguishes Islam from these two monotheistic religions. Muhammad never professed to be able to perform miracles but the Koran recognizes him as the Lord's authority on Earth, which elevated Muhammad's esteem among his followers and helped propel a new religion based heavily on the Prophet's words. "Believe in God and His messenger," the Koran says. "Obey God and obey His apostle if you would be true believers."

Muhammad fulfilled his role as messenger and preached throughout Arabia, attracting many followers. Like the founders of Judaism and Christianity, authorities in Arabia saw Muhammad as a threat to their power and forced him out of Mecca in 622 A.D. Muhammad and his followers journeyed to Medina, a sojourn that became known as the Hijrah, and marked the beginning of the Muslim calendar and the founding point of Islam. Within ten years, Muhammad and his legions returned to Mecca and conquered it.

### The Five Pillars of Islam

The Five Pillars of Islam form the main customs for Muslims, customs that guide followers of Islam toward a good and responsible life. The Five Pillars are:

- *Shahadah*: reciting Muslim revelations and submitting to God
- *Salat*: praying five times per day
- *Zakat*: donating a set portion of one's yearly income to charity, usually 2.5 percent

- *Sawm*: fasting during the month of Ramadan (the ninth month in the Muslim calendar, when Muslims seek to deepen their spirituality through self-discipline)
- *Hajj*: making a pilgrimage to Mecca at least once in one's lifetime

### Muhammad's Army

On the eve of launching his attack on Mecca in 630 A.D., Muhammad's community of believers, or *umma*, had grown considerably, making him the dominant power in Arabia. In the eight years after he and his small band of followers crept out of Mecca, Muhammad raided caravans and pagan communities throughout Arabia and converted the captured to Islam. Eventually, the ranks of Muhammad's army grew to about 10,000 men.

Two years later, Muhammad died, but his believers continued to carry the faith, which spread from the Atlantic Ocean and to Persia. Throughout their conquests, the Muslims imparted the Arabic language and culture, and virtually all the people the Muslims conquered began to think of themselves as Arabic.

### Baghdad, the Jewel of Arabia and Center for Islam

Although divisions within Islamic leadership would lead to schisms and the creation of two Islamic sects, the Sunnis (people of faith) and Shiites (contesting party), Islam flourished, especially in Baghdad. By the mid-ninth century, Baghdad was the jewel of Arabia, a wealthy commercial center renowned throughout the world for its arts, culture, and scholarship. Meanwhile, Europe plodded through its Middle Ages, no match for the Middle East's ingenuity and dynamism.

Translators and interpreters in Baghdad in a short time converted centuries of Greek writings on philosophy, medicine, and astronomy into Arabic, infusing Greek thought into the Arab culture. A small band of Arab thinkers, influenced by Greek ideals of free will and reason, began to talk about how free will and reason could coexist with Islam's strict belief that God predetermines everyone's destiny, that God has a set plan for everyone. But for whatever reason, Greek ideals never won popular support, and many Arabs opted for a far stricter form of Islam.

### The Rise of Islamic Fundamentalism

Turkey's move toward secularism in the 1920s spurred the fundamentalist movement within Islam. A few groups began to form about this time, creating a protest movement against Arab leaders who tried to secularize Middle East governments. Leaders of these groups called for *jihad*—or personal struggle—a term that has been co-opted by some radical Islamicists to mean a call for war against the West and its influences on Arab culture.

In addition, Osama bin Laden, an extremist from Saudi Arabia, is a product of this call for jihad. Bin Laden calls for a total rejection of Western culture and opposes any accommodation of Western ideals. Most scholars believe fundamentalists like those who follow bin Laden's extremism make up a small minority of the Arab population. Throughout the Middle East, most thinkers believe in a much more constructive search for Islam's place in the twenty-first century.

## SPOTLIGHT ON SAUDI ARABIA

As we saw in the beginning of this book with youths who "number" each other and date via cell phones, most Saudi Arabians struggle to combine their history and traditions with the demands of the modern world and do not identify with extremists like Osama bin Laden. Saudis attempt to navigate their world without losing sight of their traditional beliefs, despite living in one of the most traditional of all Arab societies.

### Islam's Home

Saudi Arabia is the home of Islam's holiest cities, Mecca and Medina. About 1.3 billion Muslims worldwide look to these holy lands for spiritual guidance and renewal. The country is deeply conservative and ruled by the Saud royal monarchy, which enforces strict Islamic law, or Sharia, over its approximately 24 million citizens.

Age-old Bedouin culture and nomadic traditions still resonate with many Saudis. About 600,000 Saudis still live nomadic lifestyles, while many more live semi-nomadic lives, and still other Bedouins work in offices and manage retail stores but strongly identify with Bedouin tribal customs.

While the Bedouin lifestyle and traditions are important, at the same time U.S.-style consumerism is a driving force in the Saudi Arabian economy. Many Saudis prefer American cars, the latest electronic gizmos, Western-style clothing, while its leaders own opulent homes in the United States and Europe. Saudi Arabia is also a close U.S. ally, a relationship that has made the Saudi government a target of al-Qaida.

As we've seen, Saudi Arabia is the birthplace of Osama bin Laden and 15 of the 19 September 11, 2001, hijackers; however, Saudis have also been the victims of many al-Qaida bombings and terrorist attacks. Al-Qaida militants have repeatedly bombed Saudi cities in an effort to force the country's leaders to purge all Western influences from Saudi Arabia. Despite close ties to the United States, however, Saudi leaders have shown little interest in democratic reforms.

### The Saud Ruling Family

Saudi Arabia, named after the Saud family who came to power in the 1920s, maintains an absolute monarchy and holds all power. There is neither a legislature nor political parties. The family appoints all government ministers and officials; sons in the Saud family inherit power in a royal line of succession. In the early 1990s, Saudi Arabia issued its first constitution and established a governing body call the Consultative Council but these measures have been widely viewed as political window dressing in answer to pressure from within the country and from abroad for more political freedom and choice.

Saudi Arabia's religious faith, known as Wahhabism, an austere form of Islam, greatly restricts women's rights. For example, women are strictly segregated from men in Saudi society. Women make up only 6 percent of the workforce and must work in offices segregated by sex. Schools, restaurants, and other public places are also segregated by sex as well as buses and trains. Women are not permitted to travel alone nor are they permitted to drive. However, in recent years, women have made some progress. In 2003, about half were literate, compared to 2 percent forty years earlier, and females made up half of all students in Saudi schools.

Women in Saudi Arabia who want to go to school and have careers are a good example of the issues Saudi leaders face when considering how to maintain age-old traditions in a global world. Most countries face the same pressures of globalization but maybe none more than Saudi Arabia. The Middle East has in many ways become the battleground for where globalization is fought, and Saudi Arabia sits at the center of this maelstrom. (*This section on Saudi Arabia was based on reporting by Frank Viviano for National Geographic*, 2003.)

## CONCLUSION

In the twenty-first century, the Middle East is a region still looking for its own identity. After the fall of the Ottoman Empire, for the first time in about 2,000 years, the region sought self-rule, sought to establish its own institutions, its own visions for the future. Yet for many in the region, there is a sense that the dreams and desires that accompanied freedom have gone unfulfilled. These unfulfilled dreams along with staggering problems—such as a poor education system, an underdeveloped economy, unequal distribution of wealth, and bitter conflicts—cast a malaise over daily life, leaving many to wonder what happened to a region that once held such promise.

The Middle East, after all, has made great contributions to science, art, literature, philosophy, and more and is the birthplace of societies that produced some of the world's great cultures—Arab, Jewish, Persian, and Turkish, among others. Lying at the crossroads of Asia, Africa, and Europe, the Middle East directly or indirectly impacts the lives of everyone living on the planet and is a region of critical importance. In the Middle East, cell-phone consumerism wrestles with Islamic fundamentalism and whatever direction the region chooses—

whether it decides to become a more democratic, free, and open society or chooses to remain closed—its choices will reverberate around the world and affect billions of people.

## STUDY QUESTIONS

1. What is nationalism? What forms of nationalism have sprouted in the Middle East? How did the national search for identity produce organizations like the Muslim Brotherhood and people like Osama bin Laden?

2. What are some aspects of identity? Why is Bedouin culture important to identity for many Saudi Arabians?

3. What is monotheism? What are the three monotheistic religions? How are these three religions alike? Different? Why is Judaism the story of a people and why is Israel central to Jewish identity?

4. What are the Five Pillars of Islam? How is Muhammad's relationship to Islam similar and/or different to Christ's relationship to Christianity?

5. From what you know about Western Europe in the Dark Ages, how did this region compare to Baghdad and the Middle East in the mid-ninth century?

6. In what ways have the West and East clashed in the Middle East? How does this friction still reverberate in modern times?

7. What are some of the challenges Islam poses for leaders in the Middle East in modern times? How has Islam impacted the history of the Middle East? How does it continue to impact the Middle East and the world?

# Appendix A: Middle East Time Line

**9000–8000 B.C.**
First permanent settlements appear in Canaan (modern Israel)

**8000–7000 B.C.**
Early stages in the development of agriculture

**3500 B.C.**
The threshold of civilization takes place in Mesopotamia and Egypt. Many distinct cultures in the region are connected through trade networks. Sumerians develop first writing system.

**3100–2300 B.C.**
Sumer civilization; Egypt becomes world's first country

**2300–2279 B.C.**
Akkadian Empire of Sargon I

**1800 B.C.**
Beginnings of Judaism

**1350–1300 B.C.**
Hittite Empire

**1250 B.C.**
Israelite exodus from Egypt

## 1200 B.C.

Ramses II, Egypt's greatest pharaoh, rules and extends Egypt's control from Turkey to the Sudan.

## 1004–930 B.C.

Ancient Israel; reign of kings David and Solomon

## 722–705 B.C.

Assyrian Empire under Sargon II

## 539 B.C.

Persian armies take control of Babylon, marking new era of empire in the Middle East, whereby the region as a whole is passed around from one world power to another, ending with the Ottomans in 1912.

## 334–326 B.C.

Alexander the Great subdues Egypt, overthrows the Persians, and eventually extends his empire from Eastern Europe to Hindu Kush and from northern Africa to Anatolia.

## 4th century B.C.–4th century A.D.

Greeks and Romans dominate the Middle East.

## 1st century A.D.

Christ is born; beginnings of Christianity

## 70–135 A.D.

Roman forces destroy Jerusalem. A second Jewish revolt against Romans ends with Romans exiling the Jews.

## 400 A.D.

Christianity is well established as official religion of Roman Empire.

## 7th century

Founding of Islam, the world's third monotheistic religion with Judaism and Christianity.

## 1095

Pope Urban II calls Christians to reclaim the Holy Land from Muslim and Jewish control and begins the Crusades.

## 1400–1912
Ottoman Empire takes control of North Africa, Anatolia, Nile Valley, Mesopotamia, the Balkan Peninsula, and parts of Eastern Europe and the Crimea, as well as lands ringing the Black Sea.

## 1869
Suez Canal opens.

## 1877
Jews from Europe and elsewhere begin to arrive in Palestine in growing numbers.

## 1908
Oil is discovered in Persia.

## 1917
Balfour Declaration sets out establishment of Jewish homeland.

## 1919
Ibn Saud seizes control of the Arabian Peninsula and creates Saudi Arabia.

## 1920
British and French mandates over parts of Middle East are established.

## 1927
Oil is discovered in Iraq.

## 1938
Oil is discovered in Saudi Arabia.

## 1939–1945
World War II. End of Western colonialism over the Middle East.

## 1947–1949
United Nations partition plans creating Jewish state and Arab state out of Palestine and sets control of Jerusalem. Israel declares independence in 1948, defeats Egypt, Syria, Jordan, Iraq, and Saudi Arabia in a one-year war after the countries launch an assault to stop the Israelis.

**1967**

Six-Day War erupts when Egypt invades; Israel extends control to Sinai Peninsula, Golan Heights, West Bank, and Gaza Strip.

**1979**

Islamic revolution—Western-backed Shah of Iran is dethroned and Islamic rule declared.

**1987**

Arabs launch first intifada against Israel.

**1980–1988**

Saddam Hussein of Iraq attacks Iran, fearing Islamic Revolution might spread to his country.

**1990**

Saddam Hussein annexes Kuwait.

**1991**

Coalition of armies led by the United States liberates Kuwait.

**1993**

Oslo Accords establish road map for peace in the Arab–Israeli conflict.

**2001–2003**

September 11, 2001—Al-Qaida extremists launch suicide bombings of World Trade Center and Pentagon by crashing jetliners into the buildings. Passengers thwart another suicide bombing when a hijacked plane headed for Washington, D.C., crashes in Pennsylvania.

The United States launches war against al-Qaida and al-Qaida's hosts, the Taliban, in Afghanistan. The United States, Britain, and other coalition forces launch second Gulf War in Iraq.

# Appendix B: Internet Resources

**About.com, ancienthistory.about.com**
Great resource for current as well as ancient and classical history

**Al Jazeera, english.aljazeera.net/HomePage**
English version of Al Jazeera, a Middle East television news organization, in the same vein as CNN and BBC; offers a Middle East point of view on news and happenings in the region

**The American Forum for Global Education, www.globaled.org**
Specialists in global education for about three decades, the forum provides a wealth of resources for students and educators.

**Arab.net**
Short, concise readings on individual countries and histories; also a good source for current events

**British Broadcasting Company, www.bbc.co.uk**
Great site for current events and general history; also an excellent resource for world religions

**Columbia University, www. columbia. edu/cu/lweb/indiv/mideast/ cuvlm**
All-around resource guide for the Middle East, featuring links for country resources, food, languages, bibliographies, and more

**Emayzine.com**
Dr. Eric Mayer's Web magazine for the social sciences; resources on ancient and classical history as well as modern history, and features an assortment of easy to understand lectures on a wide variety of topics

**Islamic Arts and Architecture, www.islamicart.com**
Good resource for Muslim calligraphy, art, and architecture with explanations that put the art in a historical context

**Jewish Virtual Library, www.us-israel.org**
Plethora of resources and links for modern and ancient Jewish history

**Los Angeles County Museum of Art, www.lacma.org**
Many images and explanations of art in the Middle East and elsewhere

**New York Times, www.nytimes.com**
Analysis, current events, and opinions concerning the Arab–Israeli conflict and more

**SUNY-Albany, www.albany.edu/history/middle-east/index.html**
Resources on Middle East history, society, and culture; many more links than could ever be explored in one Middle East unit

**Washington State University, www.wsu.edu:8080/~dee**
*World Civilizations: An Internet and Classroom Anthology*—excellent world history site and many links to other sites for the study of world civilizations

# Glossary

**al-Qaida:** Islamic extremist organization led by Osama bin Laden. The group is responsible for the September 11, 2001 attacks on the United States and many other terrorist bombings. The group seeks to drive Western influence out of the Middle East.

**aquifers:** underground sources of water.

**caliphs:** successors of Muhammad considered to be the spiritual head of Islam.

**Hijrah:** literally, Hijrah means migration. It refers to the journey to Medina by Muhammad and his followers in 622 A.D. after authorities in Mecca opposed Muhammad and his teachings. This journey marks the beginning of Islam and the Islamic calendar.

**horseshoe arch:** an upside down horseshoe structure vaulting over an opening or forming a domed-style ceiling. The horseshoe arch widens outward from its base before narrowing as it curves toward its apex.

**intifada:** uprising of Arabs living in the Gaza Strip and West Bank in protest of Israeli occupation. The protests began in 1987 and 2000 and have resulted in a cycle of violence, where Arabs attack and kill Israeli troops and civilians, followed by deadly retaliations by Israeli forces on Arabs.

**janissaries:** foreign soldiers fighting against the Turks who, upon being captured, later became soldiers and administrators in the Ottoman Empire.

**jihad:** a crusade undertaken in the name of Islamic beliefs. In Islam, the term originally had a more personal connotation of inner struggle but in recent times many Islamic extremists have redefined jihad as a holy war against Western nations and Western influence.

**kaffiyeh:** the band used to hold a head cloth in place.

**myrrh:** a yellowish, sticky resin obtained from trees in some parts of the Middle East.

**oasis:** lush or fertile areas in Middle East deserts where water and vegetation can be found.

**Palestine:** territory between the Jordan River and the Mediterranean Sea controlled by various peoples and empires since antiquity. The state of Israel occupies the majority of Palestine. The rest, the West Bank and the Gaza Strip, is where Israel and the Palestinian Authority exercise control.

**Palestinian Liberation Organization:** an umbrella organization of Arab groups established in 1964 and led by Yasir Arafat. The PLO represents Palestinian Arabs in their struggle with Israel for their own sovereign state. Although the PLO is not a state government, it has observer status in the United Nations and receives diplomatic recognition from over 100 countries. There are many diverse groups in the PLO. Some like Hamas, al-Fatah, and the Islamic Jihad, advocate violence and terrorism to solve the Arab–Israeli conflict.

**Sharia:** Muslim religious law based on the Koran and used by some Middle Eastern countries to govern all aspects of society from legal systems to social norms.

**ulama:** a group of learned clerics who provide guidance on a range of social and political issues.

**umma:** a community of Islamic believers; the Muslim community.

# Bibliography

Bickerton, Ian J. *A Concise History of the Arab–Israeli Conflict*. Upper Saddle River, N.J.: Prentice Hall, 2002.

*CIA World Factbook*. Washington, DC: Brassey's, 2003.

Drummond, Dorothy Weitz. *Holy Land, Whose Land? Modern Dilemma, Ancient Roots*. Seattle, Wash.: Educare Press, 2002.

Faroqhi, Suraiya. *Approaching Ottoman History: An Introduction to the Sources*. New York: Cambridge University Press, 1999.

Fromkin, David, et al. *Cradle and Crucible: History and Faith in the Middle East*. Washington, D.C.: National Geographic, 2003.

Gettleman, Marvin E., and Stuart Schaar, eds. *The Middle East and Islamic World Reader*. New York: Grove Press, 2003.

Goldschmidt, Arthur Jr. *A Concise History of the Middle East*. Boulder, Colo.: Westview Press, 1996.

Hourani, Albert. *A History of the Arab Peoples*. Cambridge, Mass.: Belknap Press of Harvard University Press, 2002.

Hudson, Michael C., ed. *Middle East Dilemma: The Politics and Economics of Arab Integration*. New York: Columbia University Press, 1999.

Kort, Michael G. *The Handbook of the Middle East*. Brookfield, Conn.: Twenty-First Century Books, 2002.

McCarthy, Justin, and Carolyn McCarthy. *Who Are the Turks?* New York: American Forum for Global Education, 2003.

McCoy, Lisa. *Facts and Figures about the Middle East*. Philadelphia, Penn.: Mason Crest Publishers, 2003.

Regional Bureau for Arab States. *Arab Human Development Report 2002*. New York: United Nations Development Program, 2002.

Sela, Avraham. *Political Encyclopedia of the Middle East*. Jerusalem: Jerusalem Publishing House, 1999.

Viviano, Frank. Kingdom on Edge: Saudi Arabia. *National Geographic Magazine*, 2003.

## *About the Author*

**Joseph D. Wilcox** is a writer living in Pittsburgh, Pennsylvania. He has a master's degree in international studies and is a former assistant program director for The American Forum for Global Education.

**The American Forum for Global Education**, a private non-profit organization founded in 1970, provides leadership to strengthen the education of our nation's youth by fostering the ability to think creatively, analytically, and systematically about issues in a global context.

120 Wall Street, Suite 2600
New York, NY 10005
Phone: 212-624-1300
E-mail: info@globaled.org
URL: www.globaled.org